Scripture: A Mirror

The Chinmaya Study Group

Published by
Chinmaya Mission West
P.O. Box 129, Piercy, CA 95587 U.S.A.
Tel. (707) 247-3488
Email: publications@chinmayamission.org
Website: www.chinmayamission.org

First Edition: December 2013, 5000 copies

Above all, deep gratitude to Pūjya Guruji. Part I of the book is based largely on his talks at the Workshop for Study Group Sevaks at Kolwan in September 2009.

Heartfelt thanks to Swamini Nishthananda for her considerable inputs; to Swamis Brahmananda, Mitrananda, and Swatmananda for facilitating research at their centers; to Swami Advayananda for clarifying doubts; and to Swami Nikhilananda and Swamini Gurupriyananda for all support. G. N. Seshadri, Vinita Asrani, Hemachandrudu Linga, and Rudite Emir offered a variety of assistance throughout the process of research and writing.

Many thanks to Ācāryas, Study Group sevaks, and others for photographs and data that have enriched this narrative. Jasjit Mansingh and Shibani Khorana were meticulous with editorial inputs, and Cauvery Bhalla was prompt with archival sources.

Special thanks to the National Museum, New Delhi, for permission to print photos of three miniature paintings.

The final touches of this book would not have been possible without the many insightful suggestions of the Mananam editorial team.

Finally, thanks to Full Circle Publishing for contributing generously its resources for the design and layout. The enthusiasm and generosity of all ensured that this effort was carried out in a true yajña spirit.

Compiled and Edited by : Anita Raina Thapan
Cover Photograph : Photographer not known

The quotes of Gurudev and related matter have been taken from the many issues of *Tapovan Prasad*, several CCMT publications, and others as indicated in the footnotes.

Printed by
Silverpoint Press Pvt. Ltd., Mumbai, India

Library of Congress Control Number: 2013942818
ISBN: 9781608270125

THE mananam SERIES
CHINMAYA BIRTH CENTENARY CELEBRATION SERIES

Scripture: A Mirror

The Chinmaya Study Group

CHINMAYA PUBLICATIONS
CHINMAYA MISSION WEST PUBLICATIONS DIVISION

IT IS TIME THAT PHILOSOPHY AND RELIGION
WALKED OUT OF OUR LIBRARIES AND TEMPLES
TO SERVE THE AGE.

| SWAMI CHINMAYANANDA |

An offering of love,
at the sacred feet
of Pūjya Gurudev,
Swami Chinmayananda

Contents

PART TWO The Forest

Multiple Voices — Individual experiences

Multiple Voices — Collective Experiences

Views, Recollections, and Reflections

Foreword

[Transcription of a talk on the Study Group by
Pūjya Guruji Swami Tejomayananda at Sidhbari, March 2011]

Our physical strength does not depend upon how much food we eat. It depends on how much food we are able to digest and assimilate. In the same way, the strength of our spiritual knowledge depends upon how much of what we hear from our teachers is absorbed. Knowledge that has been assimilated becomes part of our personality and is reflected in our actions. When I say, "I know this, but I cannot practice it," it is evident that the knowledge has remained mere information. The means for internalizing knowledge is called *mananam*, or reflection, and the Study Group is centered precisely on that.

After his jñāna yajñas, Pūjya Gurudev would advise all present to form Study Groups. He also gave them a scheme of study, so that they could go about it in a systematic manner. What is important to bear in mind is that while the jñāna yajña is for listening, the Study Group is meant for reflecting. The change in the personality comes about slowly, and the proof of it becomes evident in one's actions and attitudes.

I was once in Allahabad with Gurudev when a Mission member asked how the Study Group could be made interesting. Gurudev, in his inimitable style, said, "Take a paper and a pen," and then, after a brief pause, continued, "and invite some musicians and dancers!" The man was shocked. So was everyone else! Then, after another brief pause, Gurudev continued: "You see, if you want to make the Study Group interesting, you have to study. Only then will it become interesting, not by doing something else." That was shock therapy!

Many people are content with just śravaṇam, or the listening to discourses. The result of that is illustrated by a beautiful story from the Purāṇas. Once, a person called Gokarṇa conducted a seven-day discourse on the *Śrīmad Bhāgavatam (Bhāgavat Saptāha)*, which many people attended. At its conclusion, an airplane came from the abode of the Lord to take just one member of the entire assembly to Vaikuṇṭha, the abode of Lord Viṣṇu. Taken aback, all those present asked the pilot why only one person was chosen when so many had listened to the same discourse. The pilot replied that all had, indeed, listened to the discourse, but, thereafter, none had given a second thought to what had been heard. Everyone went home and got busy with other things. This one man, however, was in great distress. He continued thinking about what he had heard, of how to put an end to sorrow. As a result, he was able to gain the knowledge. The others had merely heard the talk.

Thereupon, Gokarṇa declared that they would have a second *Bhāgavat Saptāha*. This time, everyone in the assembly made it a point to listen attentively. At the end of the program, another airplane came and, this time, everyone was taken to Vaikuṇṭha.

This story simply illustrates that no transformation is possible without reflection. Gurudev used to give a beautiful example: if you have a cup of coffee or tea with sugar and you don't stir in the sugar, then when you sip it, the coffee or tea remains bitter or insipid. The sweetness comes only from the stirring of the sugar. In the same way, unless we assimilate all that we listen to or read, the knowledge does not get internalized, and no sweetness is reflected in our personality.

Scripture as Mirror

When you study physics, chemistry, or any other subject, your attention remains on that topic. In the same way, when I give you an object, say, a wristwatch, and you look at it, your whole attention remains on that object. If, however, I give you a mirror, then when you look into it, your attention is drawn to yourself. You become aware of the faults in your face or figure, faults that you would not appreciate having others point out to you.

Now, the subject matter of the scriptures is Self-knowledge. The śāstras tell us about our mind, thoughts, emotions, and our own true nature. They point out why and how the mind acquires impurity. What is interesting is that the scriptures don't say that we are impure. Instead, they highlight how it is only the mind that is impure.

That the scriptures act as a mirror is best illustrated by a story of the great saint Eknath Maharaj. He had a daughter who was married to a scholarly pundit. That young man developed some wrong habits and started enjoying an immoral life. The unhappy daughter complained to her father, urging him to find a solution to her misery. Eknath Maharaj assured her that all would be well. Calling his son-in-law, he mentioned how he had heard about the young man's nightlife. Without complaint or criticism, he explained that his daughter was not educated and suffered because she did not have enough dispassion toward her husband and his inclinations. Eknath Maharaj went on to suggest that the husband spend a little time with his wife every evening teaching her one or two ślokas from the *Bhagavad-gītā* before stepping out. That, he assured his son-in-law, would help considerably and take the young woman's mind off her sorrow. The son-in-law readily agreed.

The study commenced. By the time they reached the second chapter, where it is described that the senses are turbulent and even learned persons get carried away by them, the son-in-law was shocked into a new sense of self-awareness. He suddenly became aware of the fact that he was not simply teaching his wife. The *Gītā* was, as it were, holding a mirror up to him. Realizing what he was doing, he became a changed person.

This true story shows what the study of *Bhagavad-gītā* can accomplish. The study of the scriptures is like looking into a mirror. It is only when we become aware of our faults that we can be motivated to transform ourselves. Therefore, the weekly study class is very important. Preparation for that class implies daily study because, as Bhagavān Śaṅkarācārya says, *vedo nityam adhīyatām* — you must study the scripture every day. A scheme is given for systematic study that you can follow.

Daily study is a must. Just as we eat and sleep every day, so also we need to study the scriptures on a daily basis. This is because we are experts in forgetting. If we don't remain in touch with this knowledge, even for a few days, we tend to lose sight of the goal. If, on the other hand, we are reminded of it every day, it remains in our mind, constantly. The Upaniṣad declares, *svādhyāyānmā pramadaḥ* — never be negligent toward study. Certain things like prayer to God and the study of scriptures should never be forsaken even for a single day, because the mind has the tendency to slip very easily.

Studying the scripture for the assimilation of knowledge and for the consequent self-transformation is one aspect of scriptural study. However, there is also a second aspect. The *Taittirīya Upaniṣad* declares, *svādhyāyapravacanābhyāṁ na pramaditavyam* — whatever you learn must also be shared with others. Gurudev wanted everyone who attended the Study Group to also start a new Study Group after some time somewhere else, so it would have a ripple effect. Instead, what often happens is that people become so fascinated by textual study that they go on indefinitely, and just remain in a small group. Therefore, it is your duty to study for yourself, and also to share the knowledge. Don't become a guru immediately, but share what you have learned, because it is only by sharing that your knowledge gets strengthened.

Gurudev declared that he did not wish to stamp anybody as his devotee. Instead, he urged one and all to "be devoted to that knowledge." If he had any Guru-mantra to give, it was that alone.

Introduction

This is the story of Pūjya Gurudev Swami Chinmayananda's grand vision of spiritual and cultural revival of India's timeless heritage. It is also the story of the empowered householder (gṛhastha), who became a key player in the establishment and development of the Master's mission. Ruthlessly discarding beliefs and practices that had become obsolete in the modern era, Gurudev fearlessly and resolutely restored what was relevant and noble from ancient tradition. The Study Group is a modern adaptation of an ancient concept with roots in the Vedas.

The Study Group, as envisioned by Gurudev, is nothing short of a stroke of genius. With it, he created sacred learning spaces for individual and collective transformation. Through it, he ensured that scriptural knowledge, which had been the preserve of maṭhas, āśramas, and temples, reached homes, factories, schools, corporate offices, and public places. In this manner, he wove spirituality into the fabric of everyday life and made the householder the instrument for a national awakening into higher consciousness.

Totally dedicated to this knowledge, which had transformed him and led him to the ultimate state of Self-realization, Gurudev sought to make that wisdom accessible to each and every member of society. His entire work and teaching emanated from this knowledge and was for this knowledge. He inspired each one who came in contact with him to study, because through this knowledge alone could they attain lasting happiness. Through it alone could they become positive contributors to society.

The number of sannyāsīs would always be limited. The householders, however, would always constitute the great majority. While the trained, dedicated missionary would take the Master's teachings to a vast public, the devoted and inspired householder would sustain and deepen those teachings within a limited group. Householders would, therefore, be pivotal in the process of national revival. For they were teachers, soldiers, corporate leaders, administrators, and others, who shaped the values and aspirations of society. They had the power to implement policies and lifestyles inspired by the scriptures. And the platform on which this initial self-development would take place was the Study Group.

This book is divided into two parts. The first part deals with the vision of Gurudev as declared by him through numerous talks, writings, and letters. It roots the Study Group concept in the vast continuum of Indian thought and tradition, thereby highlighting its crucial role in the renaissance of Hindu culture. As Gurudev points out:

> The word 'Hindu' is universal rather than communal. He who respects and reveres the noble and the ethical values of life, who lives in self-control, whose mission in life is to end the animal in himself and regain the Kingdom of God 'within' — all such men of cultural ambition are Hindus, and there is necessarily a deep affinity of soul between such men of similar life values.

The foundations of this way of life are spelled out in the Upaniṣads and the *Bhagavad-gītā*.

The first part of this book also elaborates on the concept of the Chinmaya Study Group and the strategies adopted to make it relevant in the contemporary context. Thereafter, a brief history of the actual implementation of the idea follows. Like everything else, this concept came with its own set of rewards and challenges. The fact that the

Mission has grown into what it is today is testimony to the experiment's grand and continuing success.

The second part of this book reflects the many voices that share their stories and experiences on the journey to self-transformation. Rich in narratives from around the world, it captures how the Study Group has impacted the personal, social, and professional lives of those who have been, and those who continue to be, a part of this grassroots activity. It reflects how numerous people, through contact with the presence and teachings of Gurudev, assumed roles they had never dreamed of. They discovered their hidden potential and saw it blossom. Their lives and their work were inspired by the Divine and dedicated to the Divine. The stories of their journey and their legacy must be told, because their challenges and obstacles are no different from what successive generations will face, for the human mind does not change. Its characteristics and aspirations remain ever the same. These stories will help us better appreciate and nurture Gurudev's legacy. It will guide us in becoming, in turn, worthy instruments of the world-transforming movement he set in motion.

This second part of the book also offers an insight into the perspectives of the different protagonists who have been a part of this effort — Gurudev himself, Guruji Swami Tejomayananda, many Ācāryas, countless dedicated members of Study Groups, and others who, at some point in time, have been associated with this activity.

These stories will speak to the hearts and minds of the readers and enable them to gauge the power of this deceptively simple forum. We hope that the readers will be inspired to enroll in Study Groups, start new ones, discover hidden abilities within themselves and play their own role in the spiritualization of contemporary life.

PART ONE

The Seed

SELF-REDEMPTION MUST COME ULTIMATELY FROM OURSELVES. THE EXTERNAL PROPS SUCH AS TEMPLES, IDOLS, AND GURUS ARE ALL ENCOURAGEMENTS AND AIDS. THEY MUST BE INTELLIGENTLY USED TO HELP BUILD UP INNER PERFECTION.

| SWAMI CHINMAYANANDA |

The Vision

I

The Birth of Chinmaya Mission

June 5, 1953, marked the conclusion of Swami Chinmayananda's first yajña in Chennai and the beginning of a movement, the likes of which modern India had not witnessed before. At that point in time, however, no one could have guessed that they were witnessing a turning point in the spiritual and cultural history of contemporary India. The powerful words of the brilliant, unknown, young Swami had kindled a flame in the hearts of a group of people in Chennai. Their lives would, henceforth, never be the same again, for they had taken their first sip from the fountain of knowledge and their thirst would not be quenched.

On Swamiji's suggestion, this group of people set up an informal forum to collectively study the Upaniṣads. These texts, Swami Chinmayananda had emphasized, needed to be read numerous times for the knowledge to percolate into and be assimilated by the heart and mind. In fact, ever since the first yajña at Pune (December 31, 1951–April 8, 1952), Swami Chinmayananda had appealed to seekers to form small groups and sustain the study of Vedānta in a regular manner. He did not wish their interest to slacken once the jñāna yajña was over and they returned to their mundane lives.

Chennai, 1953. First jñāna yajña in Chennai, morning session.

Members of this group had one thing in common. All of them were educated brahmins who had grown up practicing the ritualistic aspect of the Vedas. Although they had some knowledge of the *Bhagavad-gītā*, none had ever been exposed to the profound wisdom of the Upaniṣads. Swami Chinmayananda's expounding of the *Muṇḍaka Upaniṣad* had blazed a new horizon in their lives. This exposure instantly became a compelling and driving force. This highly motivated group included G. Rangaswami Iyer (who became the Founder Secretary of Chinmaya Mission when it was established in Chennai in 1953), Sunderesa Iyer, G. Natarajan Iyer (later Swami Dayananda, no longer with the Mission), Kanti Iyer (later Swami Shantananda, not the Mission's current Swami Shantananda), Lalitha (Professor of Sanskrit at the University of Madras), M. Vasudeva Naidu, P. V. Karunakaran Nair, M. L. Leela, and P. A. Subramaniam (Professor of English at Annamalai University).

Chinmaya Mission, Chennai, 1953.

They held their first meeting at 27 Halls Road, the residence of Śrī Rangaswamy. Shortly thereafter, they moved to Sankita Nilayam, a rented house next to a temple at Egmore, Chennai.

The texts available for study were the three Upaniṣads that Swami Chinmayananda had already discoursed upon: *Kena Upaniṣad* and *Kaṭha Upaniṣad* from his first yajña at Pune, and the *Muṇḍaka Upaniṣad* which had been the topic of the second yajña held in Chennai. All three texts, with the commentary of Swami Chinmayananda, had been published as a yajña prasāda (blessing or keepsake) to ensure that they would be widely read and discussed by an ever-growing number of people.

Two months later, this group from Chennai wrote to Swami Chinmayananda in Uttarkashi in the Himalayas, seeking his permission to create a formal organization and name it Chinmaya Mission. They stressed that an organization was required to provide a formal platform for the systematic study of the scriptures. A reply soon arrived:

> Don't start any organization in my name. I've not come here to be institutionalized. I've come here to give the message of our ancient sages, which has benefited me. If it has benefited you, pass it on.

The enthusiastic group wrote back insisting that, since the term "Chinmaya" signified "true knowledge" and "pure Consciousness," which was precisely what all of them were seeking, the name "Chinmaya Mission" was, indeed, most apt. It was to be a movement dedicated to the spread of knowledge. Thus, on August 8, 1953, Chinmaya Mission was born — the first initiative of the first Study Group.

If Swami Chinmayananda had a divine mission to awaken Indians to this great knowledge at a national level, the first Study Group set in motion a simultaneous effort of achieving the same goal at the local level. Within two years, there were six Chinmaya Mission centers in Chennai itself, each with a small spiritual library and a program of weekly discussion. Besides the study of texts, additional activities included chanting of the texts, singing of bhajans, and group meditations. All these facets of spiritual life had been included in the early yajñas of Swami Chinmayananda, and they became a part of the weekly meetings of the newly formed Chinmaya Mission.

The effect was contagious, and, soon, similar groups formed in Kerala, Bengaluru, and elsewhere, giving rise to little islands of spiritual force in the vast sea of ignorance. The Study Group was thus a direct result and follow-up of the jñāna yajña. It nurtured inspiration and gave shape to noble aspirations. Study Group members eventually took the initiative to organize Gurudev's jñāna yajñas, conduct Bala Vihars and Yuva Kendra groups, and create more Study Groups.

They arranged for the publication of Gurudev's numerous talks in book form and administered the ever-increasing number of Chinmaya Mission centers around India, and, later, abroad. The Mission quickly took root.

Thus began a renaissance of Hindu culture that was going to span several generations. It was going to open new vistas in the lives of a steadily growing number of people, without any pomp and show. It was a subtle process that would operate unseen in the hearts of individuals. It would be a slow and steady process, bringing with it a complete and lasting transformation. It would represent the efforts of multiple groups of individuals, inspired by and devoted to scriptural knowledge and the modern Ṛṣī who made it accessible to them. These groups could not fully fathom the grand vision of their Master at that point. But they had faith, commitment, and devotion, and their numbers would continue to swell steadily.

II

The Chinmaya Study Group

Group study offers a greater depth and a wider perspective to the understanding of a topic than an individual can hope to attain on his own. The group synergy not only sustains collective and individual motivation but also enables bonding and team effort, which enrich the individual, the group, and the organization. It is for this reason that the group study is common in academic and other learning environments.

The Chinmaya Study Group, however, is distinct for a variety of reasons. Above all, it is devoted to the study of the scriptures — of Advaita Vedānta in particular. Since the scriptures are concerned with the inner world of an individual, the purpose of such study is self-transformation. Hence, the goal of the Study Group is not the attainment of anything in the outside world, but rather the inner ability to better face the world and its manifold challenges.

The Study Group is a forum where intellectual knowledge must go hand in hand with devotion. Both constitute the two wings of the bird of wisdom and are necessary to enable it to soar high into the realm of experience. Mere intellectual growth invariably leads to arrogance. Common everyday experience shows how those with knowledge exploit those without it — hence, the saying, 'Knowledge is power.' However, the knowledge that the scriptures talk about leads to wisdom. Wisdom lies in the recognition that well-being can never be restricted to an individual or a group of individuals. It implies the well-being of all, for it is based on the understanding of the underlying unity of all life. Diversity exists only at the apparent, superficial level.

The Study Group is also a forum where no member is the teacher. The sole teacher is either Gurudev Swami Chinmayananda or Guruji Swami Tejomayananda whose commentary of the text is under study. The moderator of the group is one among equals. However, he or she is expected to have a little more experience and exposure to Vedānta than the others in order to be able to provoke meaningful discussion and ensure that it remains within the context of the readings.

The Chinmaya Study Group is, by and large, a neighborhood activity. The ideal size is from eight to ten people, of whom one is the moderator or facilitator. Members of the group gather in a home once a week for an hour-and-a-half to study the scriptures. In some places, Study Groups also meet at the local Mission center in smaller or bigger groups. They follow a syllabus that was set up by Gurudev and to which Guruji has added a certain number of new texts in recent years. This prescribed syllabus permits a gradual and systematic immersion into an ocean of knowledge.

No special qualifications are required to join the Study Group other than a desire for this knowledge, commitment, and dedication. There is no financial transaction involved either, for the sharing of this knowledge is itself a scriptural injunction. The ideal candidate could be one who recognizes that, despite having everything, a sense of fulfillment and plenitude is absent. Or it may be an individual propelled by some sorrow or deception to seek a deeper meaning to life. Often it is the question of one's purpose in life that arises in the mind and compels one to seek an answer. It could also be disgust at the way in which one has led one's life and a burning desire to turn over a new leaf. The Study Group is also ideal for someone who is simply interested in studying Vedānta in a structured manner with like-minded people.

The scriptures emphasize that only one-fourth of our knowledge is acquired from the teacher, who is the basic prerequisite to learning. Even today when we have access to knowledge through DVDs or over the internet, that knowledge comes from a source and that source is the teacher. A second quarter of our knowledge is gained through our own thinking and reflection. The third quarter comes about through discussion with companions, co-students, and like-minded people. The last quarter is learned through personal experiences in life, both good and bad. All these four aspects of learning are essential if one is to acquire a holistic understanding of a subject.

Highlighting the importance of the Study Group, Gurudev explained:

> Merely listening to my yajñas will not add to your beauty. These ideas are to be reflected on deeply and digested slowly. This process is hastened only when you discuss what you have studied with others. Study Groups constitute the heart of our Mission. The ideas gathered by you, when discussed with others, not only become deeply rooted in you but, as they become clearer in your own concept, in your own understanding, they also inspire those who listen to you. Thus, each student, while trying to strengthen his own understanding, can become an instrument for the spread of this knowledge. This process is the dynamic study scheme followed in the Vedāntic tradition. This is not a Chinmaya methodology; it is the most ancient Vedāntic tradition of study.

An understanding of the place of discussion in the Vedāntic tradition is, therefore, relevant at this point.

III

Discussion in the Vedāntic Tradition

Discussion in the Vedic Period

Learned men and sages in the Vedic period sharpened their thinking skills and sought clarity through interaction and questioning. Philosophers from the six schools of philosophy, who accepted the authority of the Vedas (*āstika*),[1] had rich and meaningful conversations with each other. While agreeing on many points, they also debated on subtle points of difference. The arguments with the heterodoxy, or *nāstika* schools of philosophy, which did not accept the authority of the Vedas, namely, Jainism, Buddhism, and the Cārvāka, were, however, more vigorous and contentious.

Uttara Mīmāṁsā, or Vedānta, one of the six āstika schools of philosophy, deals with the topic of Brahmavidyā, or knowledge of the nature of Brahman. The term 'mīmāṁsā' means deep reflection, inquiry, examination, and investigation. The term 'mīmāṁsāka' signifies one who investigates or inquires intensely. Inquiry and investigation imply questioning and discussion. In fact, a variety of discussion and argument styles are reflected in the vast body of scriptural literature.

The first kind of discussion in the Vedāntic tradition is *vāda*. It

1 Yoga, Sāṅkhya, Nyāya, Vaiśeṣika, Mīmāṁsā, and Uttara Mīmāṁsā, or Vedānta.

is a discussion or an argument, heated or normal, between two or more learned persons. In it, both the *vādī* (exponent) and *prativādī* (opponent) try to establish their own positions and refute that of the other with logic and quotations from authoritative sources. What is important, however, is that the aim of vāda is the discovery of Truth. It is not a mere intellectual exercise. Since the topic of the Upaniṣads is knowledge of the Self, or of the Supreme Reality, all knowledge must culminate in Self-realization. Therefore, intellectual knowledge is only the means — the most vital means — to the goal and not the goal itself.

The *Chāndogya Upaniṣad* (Chapter 5) offers a good example of vāda. Here, a group of great householders, adept in the Vedas, seek to understand the meditation on the Self as Vaiśvānara (the consciousness in all). So, they approach King Aśvapati, renowned for his knowledge of that particular meditation. The latter begins by asking each one what he meditates upon. As each describes his focus of meditation — sun, space, heaven, earth, air, and so on — the king listens attentively. Each member of the group, as it turns out, is only meditating on one aspect of the supreme Self. So the King explains the benefits that accrue from such meditation. This exchange is, therefore, both a teaching and a discussion. King Aśvapati leads the discussion through his questions, and the learned householders gain clarity on the topic through their interaction with him. The end result is complete clarity for the whole group.

The second kind of discussion in the Vedic tradition is *jalpa*. Here, a person tries to demolish the arguments of the opponent, using appropriate means of knowledge in order to establish his own standpoint or theory. In this method, the desire to win is stronger than the desire to know the truth! Jalpa, therefore, is wrangling discussion or debate, not a peaceful sharing of knowledge.

The *Bṛhadāraṇyaka Upaniṣad* (Chapter 3) offers an example of *jalpa*, which takes place in King Janaka's court. The story goes that

Janaka once conducted a yajña and distributed generous gifts. Many learned brahmins were present on the occasion. Seeing such an august gathering, the king was curious to know who among the group was the most learned and eloquent in Vedic knowledge. So, he had a thousand cows gathered and ordered twenty measures of gold to be tied to the horns of each one. He then announced that anyone in the assembly who claimed to be the greatest Vedic scholar of all could take away the thousand cows as a gift.

For a few moments, there was stunned silence in the court. Then, the sage Yājñavalkya came forth and instructed his brahmacārī to take charge of the cows. At this, many in the learned assembly took offense and challenged the claim of Yājñavalkya. The text goes on to describe how the first one to confront the sage is Aśvalāyana, the family guru of King Janaka. Shooting a volley of questions at Yājñavalkya, he seeks to disprove the former's claim. However, Yājñavalkya is able to answer the questions convincingly, and, finally, having nothing further to say, Aśvalāyana sits down. Thereafter, several brahmins stand up and pose questions to Yājñavalkya, hoping, thereby, to disqualify him. One after another, Yājñavalkya addresses their questions with reason, clarity, and conviction. Then Gārgī raises questions, in response to which Yājñavalkya elucidates on *brahmatattva*, or the knowledge of the Truth. Like the others before her, Gārgī, too, cannot disprove Yājñavalkya's supremacy.

Each member of the learned assembly sought to demolish the arguments of Yājñavalkya, using appropriate means of knowledge. The desire to defeat him was stronger than the desire to know the truth. What is significant, however, is that the audience in the assembly, listening to this exchange, would have certainly gained some deep insights into the profound questions of life. Similarly, several centuries later, we continue to learn from that very discussion.

In this manner, vāda and jalpa are employed in the scriptures as a means of explaining the great doctrine of Advaita Vedānta. The third form of discussion is *vitaṇḍā,* which is mentioned in the *Nyāyasūtras* (1.1.3) of Gautama (550 B.C.E.). Here, the opponent does not try to establish his own position but continues refuting that of the exponent. For all practical purposes, vitaṇḍā is destructive criticism. This form of argumentation was, perhaps, more prevalent between rival schools of thought in the millennium before the Christian era. Competition between the various schools was intense during their formative years, especially between 800 B.C.E. to 200 C.E. Some like the Jain, Buddhist, and Advaita schools survived, while others like Sāṅkhya did not, either getting assimilated into other schools or becoming extinct.

Scholarly disputations and philosophical discussions in the Vedic period were held not only in the palaces of great kings but also in yajñaśālās, where sages and gurus often gathered for discussion on the finer points of the scriptures. Or they were held in the pāṭhaśālās where brahmacārīs, or students, lived, pursuing the study of the scriptures. The presence of large groups of students implies discussion, even though the Upaniṣads are not explicit about this.

Discussion in the Post-Vedic Period

There are two ways in which discussions proceed in Indian scriptural literature. Either a discussion takes place between two persons, usually with a large number of people listening in and benefitting from the discussion as seen earlier in the example of the sage Yājñavalkya, or the discussion proceeds through stories within stories. This is common in the post-Vedic period in texts like the dharmaśāstras, the epics, and the Purāṇas.

In the *Manu Smṛti*, for example, Manu is asked by some sages about the dharma of different categories of people. He begins by telling them that answers to their questions were given to him once by Svayambhū Brahmā. He then passed on the knowledge to the sage Bhṛghu, who then propagated it widely. So the *Manu Smṛti* that is available to us today is thanks to the efforts of Bhṛghu. What is significant, though, is that Bhṛghu did not take active steps to teach this knowledge to anyone. Many sages, all Masters in their own right, came to him with questions, and he simply answered their questions by sharing his knowledge with them. They, in turn, shared it with their students and, in this manner, the knowledge was propagated to future generations. Thereafter, it became law. So what originated as a discussion among great sages became law for ordinary people like us.

The Purāṇas are also full of stories within stories. In the *Śrīmad Bhāgavatam*, for example, Suta Purāṇika narrates the *Bhāgavatam* to the sage Śaunaka. He claims that he is narrating it in exactly the same way that Śukadeva had earlier narrated it to King Parīkṣita. Now, whereas Śukadeva's telling of the story to Parīkṣita is a teaching, Suta Purāṇika's narration of the same to other sages is a sharing of knowledge. In this instance, the sharing happens in the intervals between different rituals associated with a grand and prolonged yajña. It is, thus, a collective study of age-old wisdom repeated to those who derive great joy from listening to it over and over again. The format is of one person talking, while others are listening. When anyone has a doubt, he is free to ask questions; if anyone among the group wishes to share something, he

Sukadevji telling the story of the Śrīmad Bhāgavatam *to Raja Parikshit and others. Rajathan, India, circa 1757.* Wikipedia.

can do so. What is noteworthy is the fact that no one person claims to be the author of a story, nor the original source of this wisdom.

In the epics (*Rāmāyaṇa* and *Mahābhārata*), there are dialogues and discussions in every conceivable human condition. Whereas, in the Upaniṣads, the topic is Brahmavidyā; in the epics, the topic is dharma. The focus is on relationships, on what is happiness and unhappiness, wealth and poverty, truth and untruth. Every question concerning the human condition begins with a personal question as an individual seeks to understand his, or her, specific situation. However, the purpose of the discussion is to throw light on the ultimate goal of life — mokṣa. This goal can only be reached by following dharma.

Whereas, in Vedic literature, the conversations are between highly learned and evolved persons, in the epics the scope is much wider. While there are dialogues and discussions between sages and kings in a royal assembly, there are other conversations between father and son, between mother and son, between friends, between commoners, between conqueror and the defeated, and between husband and wife. While some conversations are brief, others extend over several days. The longest of all conversations is between the dying Bhīṣma, lying on his bed of arrows, and Yudhiṣṭhira, who would be king.

Bhishma Pitamah on the bed of arrows. Kangra-Sikh mixed style, 19th century A.D. *Courtesy National Museum, New Delhi.*

The Krishna-Arjuna dialogue, Kangra, Pahari, circa A.D. 1800–1810.
Courtesy National Museum, New Delhi.

The best-known dialogue, however, is the one in the *Bhagavad-gītā* between Lord Kṛṣṇa and Prince Arjuna on the battlefield of Kurukṣetra. Such a dialogue between a Guru and disciple is called a *saṁvāda* and it represents a fourth form of discussion. In the *Bhagavad-gītā*, Arjuna poses numerous questions to his Guru, Śrī Kṛṣṇa, pertaining to the many dilemmas of life. Śrī Kṛṣṇa responds to each question with compassion and love, steadily taking Arjuna to unimaginable heights of spiritual experience.

Discussion from the Time of Ādi Śaṅkara to the Modern Era

In the eighth century C.E., Ādi Śaṅkara, the great spiritual reformer, spearheaded a great revival of Vedāntic wisdom, largely through discussion and debate. According to the accepted philosophical tradition in India, such debates helped to establish a new philosopher, and also to win disciples and converts from other schools. It was also the tradition for the loser of the debate to become a disciple of the winner. The most important among those that Śaṅkara defeated in debate was Viśvarūpa, the great Vedic ritualist, sometimes identified as Maṇḍana Miśra. The latter, after conceding defeat, was ordained as a sannyāsī and named Sureśvara. Sureśvarācārya, as he eventually came to be known, became the first head of the Sringeri Maṭha, one of the four maṭhas established by Śaṅkara and with which Chinmaya Mission is affiliated.

The tradition of discussion between philosophers of different schools of thought attained a new avatāra in the court of the Mughal Emperor Akbar in the sixteenth century. The latter invited representatives of all the existing faiths in India to his court for a discussion on the similarities and differences between them. In addition to the many representatives of Indian schools of thought, the group included those of faiths that had been brought to India by foreign merchants, traders, and conquerors. They included Muslims, Jesuits, Jews, Orthodox Christians, and Sufis, among others. These gatherings were perhaps the first interfaith dialogues in the world, and it is significant that they should have taken place in India where such an open mind-set had been meticulously cultivated and nurtured through the centuries.

In this way, a practice that was intrinsic to the Vedic way of life has continued to find expression in the long course of Indian history. At its origin, this tradition was never the exclusive preserve of men. Moreover, such discussions frequently crossed the barriers of class and caste. The right to question was never restricted to a particular age or stage in life. Naciketa of *Kaṭha Upaniṣad* is just a child, and yet he fearlessly asks Lord Yama, the greatest secrets of life. Similarly, Āruṇi and Śvetaketu are names of children we learn about in the scriptures; they wanted to know the truth ardently. No one discouraged them.

In the contemporary context and, more specifically, within the framework of the Vedāntic tradition, discussion and debate by scholars of the scriptures in an organized manner is restricted to a few institutions.

The Sringeri Maṭha (Śāradā Pīṭha), for example, hosts a number of conferences called *Vidvat Sadas*, or discussion forums, for Vedic scholars. This represents an unbroken tradition since the time of Ādi Śaṅkara. One such event hosted during the Vināyaka Caturthī festival, for example, lasts for about twelve days and is held in the presence of the Jagadguru Śaṅkarācārya of Sringeri. Invitation to this forum is extended to about fifty of the brightest Vedic scholars across the country. The Śāradā Pīṭha also organizes a special five-day annual śāstra sadas at the birthplace of Ādi Śaṅkara in Kerala on his birth anniversary.

While such events are important for upholding Vedic scholarship, they, nevertheless, cater to an extremely limited audience. The systematic study of the scriptures in a language and context accessible to the common educated individual had no forum in an independent and resurgent India. Modern secular education completely ignores the spiritual dimension of life in its curriculum. And yet, it was precisely that spiritual knowledge which had been the foundation of India's greatness in centuries gone by. Modern Indians had lost their moorings and needed to connect with their spiritual roots while making progress in the material world. It was precisely for these reasons that Gurudev conceived of the Study Group to fill this vacuum in society.

IV

The Empowered Gṛhastha

Swami Tapovan Maharaj, the Guru of Swami Chinmayananda, wrote:

> The śrutis and the smṛtis amply prove that in the past it was householders, more than sannyāsīs, who worked in the field of philosophical thought. Indifference to worldly pleasures is the chief requisite for spiritual advancement. Whether a man dwells at home or in the forest, if he has *vairāgya* (dispassion), he is a sannyāsī. One may put on the saffron gown and go on mumbling the mantras, but he is no sannyāsī unless he has true vairāgya. There seems to be nothing absurd in the idea of a householder immersing himself or herself in Divine thought even as the great Ṛṣīs in their Himalayan āśramas did, provided he or she has the necessary viveka (discrimination) and vairāgya.[2]

Attaining such a state of vairāgya, as described by Swami Tapovan Mahārāja, is no easy task for the modern householder. Indeed, there are only a few who would even aspire to it. Nevertheless, what is important is that this state is, indeed, attainable by those with a sincere aspiration for it, who persevere in their sādhanā, remain steadfast in their devotion to the Lord, and who have the Guru's Grace.

---

[2] Swami Tapovan, *Wanderings in the Himalayas*, p. 165.

The Householder in the Vedic Period

Uttarkashi, 1956. Swami Tapovan Maharaj

The ancient Ṛṣīs were married and had children. Yet, as highly enlightened people, they were the guides of society, and they dedicated their entire life to spreading the Vedic culture. The family was never considered an obstacle to spiritual life. The Vedas emphasize that members of the family are all a part of the integral journey. The scriptures are full of stories of highly evolved householders. Śrī Rāma, even though an avatāra, came as a householder and established inspiring ideals that householders down the ages have strived to attain. King Janaka of Mithilā exemplified how involvement with wife, children, subjects, and kingdom did not necessarily imply bondage. The court with its pleasures or the throne with its responsibilities did not affect his deep spiritual wisdom.

Enlightened householders like King Janaka were the products of an education in which the Vedas constituted the foundation of all knowledge. Such education was a combination of both spiritual and secular knowledge. The aim of Hindu culture is spiritual perfection, and the four āśramas, or stages of life, together represent a gradual evolution to this state. Since, for the average individual, the path to perfection is through the world, the guide, at every stage, is the scripture, and the daily study of it ensures that there is constant preparation for the next stage.

The scriptures, however, emphasize that this evolution from one āśrama to another may be bypassed by one in whom true dispassion arises. Such an individual, whether in the brahmacarya, the gṛhastha, or the vānaprastha stage, may then directly go to sannyāsa āśrama. Needless to say, such people represent the exceptions rather than the norm.

In the brahmacarya āśrama, the study of the Vedas is required to gain clarity on how to live life and understand one's duties. In the gṛhastha āśrama, the study is to remind oneself of the attitude toward the many duties and responsibilities of the household, community, and nation, and also to keep in mind the ultimate goal of life. In vānaprastha, the third āśrama, scriptural study is the means to gain single-pointedness of attention and for the cultivation of the six virtues[3] necessary to become a full-time seeker of Truth. Finally, the sannyāsa āśrama is devoted solely and completely to the gaining of Self-knowledge. Indian literature is full of examples of kings renouncing kingdoms to seek knowledge from a Guru, or householders renouncing home and children to live in the forest in spiritual pursuit.

All householders were enjoined to spread this knowledge to others, by both their words and their actions. The Vedic sages, therefore, did not feel the need for a special class of teachers, or sannyāsīs, for this missionary work. It was made the responsibility of every householder, as the Upaniṣads clearly emphasize that the goal of every student is to be able, in his lifetime, to train and perfect the next generation.

Access to Knowledge in the Time of Śaṅkara and Thereafter

Ādi Śaṅkara's revivalist movement in the eighth century C.E. came over twelve hundred years after the rise of Buddhism and Jainism and the steady decline of Vedic culture over the centuries. Śaṅkara was born in a period when mere ritualism had gained precedence over genuine learning and the striving for an understanding of the

---

[3] These virtues are *śama, dama, uparatī, titīkṣā, śraddhā,* and *samādhāna.* Together, they are called the six treasures (*ṣad-sampattī*).

scriptural Truth. Cultural decadence expressed itself in a variety of new forms of religious practices that had no sanction in the Vedas. Against this background, Śaṅkarācārya successfully established Advaita Vedānta as the most important pan-Indian school of thought and gave a new impetus to Vedic study and its corresponding cultural norms. To sustain and promote this achievement, he established four maṭhas and created ten orders of sannyāsīs. The focus of Vedic study, which had been the yajñaśālā and the gurukula in the Vedic period, now shifted to the maṭhas. Sannyāsīs became the custodians of this knowledge.

The maṭhas established by Ādi Śaṅkara became renowned centers of learning for centuries thereafter. However, this learning was accessible to only a limited segment of society. Moreover, Ādi Śaṅkara's teachings were addressed to religious preachers, philosophers, and thinkers of his day and not to the common man. Women and the lower castes had no access to this knowledge. They had access only to the essence of the Vedas, offered by the Purāṇas or the epics, and, that, too, only on a part-time basis, through the medium of stories. They were deemed as being incapable of understanding the mystic utterances of the Upaniṣads.

Over the centuries, for a variety of reasons, a decline in the mind-set of people set in, which was further hastened in the colonial period. Because of a lack of patronage for traditional education, Vedānta came to be recognized as the special privilege of sannyāsīs and a few brahmins. With this evolved the erroneous belief that the study of the Upaniṣads would make a healthy normal individual lose interest in life and lure him away into becoming a renunciate. This fear remains prevalent even today when men remain fearful of wives taking to this knowledge whole-heartedly, or of parents feeling alarmed when their children show enthusiasm for the study of the scriptures. They are ignorant of the fact that this very knowledge had enabled a stable family environment and a secure community life in the Vedic period.

Gurudev's Vision for the Householder

Gurudev's work in the twentieth century was as revolutionary and as wide in scope as Śaṅkara's revivalist movement had been twelve centuries earlier. In one radical sweep, Gurudev broke down age-old barriers of the mind. In his scheme of things, the jñāna yajña replaced the maṭha, the Sandeepany institutes of Vedānta became the gurukula for the modern sannyāsī, and the Study Group became the gurukula for the householder. Through this scheme, he ensured that spiritual knowledge flowed to every section of society, bringing it new life and vigor.

Indians had long forgotten that the pursuit of spiritual knowledge had for centuries been intrinsic to the culture of India. In fact, the Sanskrit term for India, 'Bhārata,' itself signifies this attitude: 'Bhā' means light or knowledge and 'rata' signifies 'being devoted.' From the earliest of times, Indians had been devoted to knowledge and made the quest for it their highest purpose of life. Gurudev brought back this value for knowledge to a society newly liberated from colonial rule and centuries of ignorance and apathy.

> This is the time for the culture of the Ṛṣīs to bring hope and strength, faith and courage, to dying hearts and confused heads.
>
> Swami Chinmayananda

The number of educated people in India in the twentieth century was higher than ever before in the country's history. The educated elite had been groomed in a system of education developed by the British. Spiritual knowledge had no place in it, but the study of science created a questioning mind in the educated. Such a questioning mind had been an indispensable tool in the traditional scheme of education, and Gurudev set to use it to great advantage for teaching the timeless science of life.

The mystical language of the Upaniṣads, as also the language of Ādi Śaṅkara's bhāṣyas, or commentaries, on them, is difficult to understand. The texts are in Sanskrit and they address the rational, thinking mind. By the twentieth century, even the Purāṇas had become inaccessible to large sections of society. Sanskrit studies had shrunk to an all-time low. In his jñāna yajñas, Gurudev simplified the commentaries on these ancient texts for the average educated person who was not necessarily a thinker or philosopher. He made Vedic knowledge accessible to all those who sought it by bringing it to the doorstep of the modern Indian, regardless of age, gender, or community.

The Study Group was conceived by Gurudev as a forum for those engaged in professional and family lives. The weekly commitment would ensure the connection with the teaching and the teacher. It would be a constant reminder of ideas and concepts gained, which would slowly transform into a refrain amid the daily chores and commitments. As more and more people made this knowledge their own, it would undoubtedly translate into a higher level of consciousness not only at home and the workplace but also spill over into the public sphere. The process would take several generations, but it was the only way to bring about a new world order.

The ancient Ṛṣīs judged the greatness of a state not by the extent of its empire or by the size of its wealth, but by the degree of righteousness and justice that marked the public administration and the private lives of its citizens. True progress was judged by spiritual and moral standards, not by material and physical ones. Sacrifice was deemed far more important than success, and renunciation was regarded as the crowning achievement of the human being. These were precisely the values and attitudes that Gurudev sought to bring back to society, for, somewhere embedded in the collective memory of people, this knowledge lay dormant as a seed. It needed watering and nurturing before it would sprout and grow.

Scheme of Unfoldment for the Householder

Gurudev referred to his householder devotees as "white-clothed sādhus" and deemed it necessary to engage them on a large scale. As he explained:

> Śaṅkara had to deal with only the highest intellectuals of his time who were also sincere in their convictions. But now, to quell the doubters of the wisdom of your religion, you have to take it to the doorsteps and into their homes in order to make them live the fragrant life that is theirs. It is not their fault. It is the fault of the times, of the situation in which the modern man finds himself. Innumerable problems confront man, intimately connecting him and affecting his day-to-day, moment-to-moment life. A growing population, cutthroat competition, and an appalling food shortage are baffling the thinking man today. In these conditions, moral values and political ideas are subjected to terrific stress and strain, and people are not prepared even to look at fresh concepts or ideas on these matters.
>
> *They* will not seek *your* message. *You* will have to take it to *them*, in a way they can assimilate it.

To set the ball rolling for the renaissance of an entire society, Gurudev began with the householders, and then gradually elaborated a study scheme for every age group, each with its own specific focus. A national revival on the scale that Gurudev envisioned required the engagement of each and everyone, according to his or her capacity. Empowerment through spiritual knowledge is the priceless gift that Gurudev gave his generation. That is the gift that Chinmaya Mission continues to offer to one and all.

Concept and Strategy

V

Relevance of Scriptural Study

Vedānta is the science of life. Unlike other sciences that pertain to aspects of the outside world, Vedānta focuses on the Self. It is concerned with the purification and upliftment of the mind. Its purpose is to lead one to Self-realization, that is, a state of liberation from all sense of limitation and finitude. As Guruji Swami Tejomayananda emphasizes, "Knowing about the world is *important*. Knowing oneself is *vital*."

The scriptures declare that we are sat-cit-ānanda — of the nature of Existence–Knowledge–Bliss, an epithet for Brahman. Initially, this remains a purely intellectual concept, for it cannot be experienced through the five senses and the mind. However, because the scriptures enable a prolonged reflection on one's own state of mind, one gradually gains clarity on what this concept really implies.

Initially comes the realization that all joy and sorrow, hope and despair, spring from the mind. It is the mind that propels us to run after sense objects in the quest of happiness. The very desire for these various objects arises because of a lack of understanding of our own true Nature. We mistakenly believe that we are the body, the mind, and the intellect, and that by satisfying these aspects of our personality, we shall attain happiness. However, we discover that such happiness is fleeting, and we are again very quickly consumed by desire. And so the cycle continues endlessly. Sustained happiness eludes us.

As we continue to study and reflect, the scriptures make us aware of the qualities that make up our mind and which propel us to behave the way we do. These qualities are *sattva* (knowledge associated with serenity), *rajas* (activity associated with agitation), and *tamas* (inertia characterized by dullness). All these three qualities exert their influence on us at different times as expressions of our vāsanās, or deep-rooted inclinations and tendencies. These vāsanās constitute the blueprint of our personality. They spring up as desires in the intellect, which then trigger off thoughts in the mind, which ultimately translate into actions at the level of the body.

To ensure noble thoughts and actions, we have to create noble vāsanās. Because the scriptures teach us *what* to think and *how* to think, the seeker is able to slowly develop the qualities and inclinations that are vital for spiritual progress. When sattva dominates our system, all the divine virtues gather within us. Noble thoughts and actions become spontaneous.

It is for this reason that the evolution of the mind is the very essence of all spiritual reformation in life. The process begins with an understanding of why we think and behave the way we do. Only then can we know what to change and how to change. The scriptures enable us to get to the root of the problem through Self-knowledge.

Self-knowledge enables us to have the right relationship with everyone and everything in life. It reveals to us the changing nature of things and beings so that we can have a wise relationship with them and not depend on them for lasting happiness. As the mind's questions find answers in the scriptures, the mind gradually grows quiet. And it is only in a silenced mind that the Truth, beyond the mind, is reflected.

1959. Preparing publications to facilitate the spread of knowledge.

The study of Vedānta is also relevant because it influences the choices we make in everyday life. It forms the basis of all moral and ethical values. In other words, it is the foundation of dharma and hence the bedrock of all religions. Unfortunately, most people understand religion to mean a code of conduct and modes of worship, rituals, and ceremonies. The differences between the various religions are basically at this level. However, if one goes more deeply into the subject, one realizes that there is a reason for the many rituals and ceremonies. Vedānta provides the logic for these customs and practices and permits the deepest understanding of human psychology.

The scriptures offer a vision of life that is holistic and all-inclusive.

Most of us have only a partial vision of life and, therefore, remain limited in some way or another. It is precisely because of this partial vision that we see the differences rather than the similarities between people. In the *Rāmāyaṇa,* Mantharā and Kaikeī are examples of a partial vision. They seek to create a rift between Śrī Rāma and his brother Bharata. The two brothers, on the other hand, have a holistic vision and remain uninfluenced by Kaikeī's demands.

The scriptures also show us how to translate the vision of oneness into action. For example, in the *Bhagavad-gītā,* Śrī Kṛṣṇa represents spiritual vision, while Arjuna is the one who translates that vision into action. The *Gītā* concludes with the declaration that, when vision is combined with action, then success, wellbeing, and victory are assured. The study of the scriptures, therefore, enables the development of a holistic vision, while providing inspiration to implement that vision in daily life, thus leading to a state of complete fulfillment and wellbeing.

The vision of oneness does not imply treating all names and forms in exactly the same way. The scriptures point out that, although all beings merit equal respect, at the transactional level, they require different treatment. For instance, love and respect for women does not imply the same familiarity with all women, as one would have with a mother, wife, or daughter. Therefore, a transaction depends upon the name, form, type of action, authority, and, finally, on saṁskāras. For purposes of transaction, tradition must be followed.

The scriptures will always remain relevant because the essential nature of life does not change. It is only the context in which we live that changes. By inculcating in the Study Group members the habit of daily study, Gurudev sought to ensure that the scriptures remain their lifelong guides.

VI

Aims and Objectives of the Study Group

Developing an inquiring, reflective mind is the first objective of the Study Group. Those who listened to Gurudev Swami Chinmayananda's discourses were at the very first stage of the spiritual journey — that of śravaṇam, or listening, to the words of the Master. Some listened in wonderment and then awaited a second such opportunity. A few, however, wanted more right away. They were the ones who were guided by Gurudev to the Study Group. They thus crossed into the second stage of spiritual practice — the process of mananam, or reflection.

Mananam is reflection upon what one has heard and read in the scriptures. Through it, clarity of vision increases and the ability to express one's convictions improves. In his commentary on *Vivekacūḍāmaṇi* (v. 365), Gurudev says:

> Knowledge can be obtained by 'listening' to a Teacher. Reading books is also a method of 'listening' to acquire knowledge. But when one sits down and reflects upon the ideas gathered from a teacher or from a book and makes them one's own, that understanding is a hundred times more powerful than what can be gained by merely 'listening' to a teacher or reading books.

Discussion with others is also a part of mananam. Gurudev elaborates in his commentary on *The Holy Gītā* (X.9):

> When students with a common intellectual interest come together and discuss among themselves their pet subject, they not only crystallize their knowledge, but often achieve a reassuring degree of confident knowledge in place of what was till then some stray information gathered from silent books. This technique of common discussion has been tirelessly emphasized in Vedānta in its very definition of Brahma-vidyā, which it upholds as one of its most important limbs of sādhanā.

Intellectual analysis and reasoning, though indispensable, do not by themselves translate into Self-realization. They do not free one from the many vagaries of the mind. The pull of the vāsanās remains strong, and the seeker feels the frustration of knowing that a wide chasm exists between what he or she knows and what he or she seeks to experience. The sense of doership, the sense of enjoyership, desire, fear, anger, and so on, remain obstacles on the path to final liberation.

This implies that mananam must lead to the third stage, that of nididhyāsana, or meditation, if it is to be a tool for total Self-transformation. The purpose of meditation is to remove the habitual wrong thinking that one is the body, mind, and intellect (BMI). Here, the seeker consciously focuses on the single thought 'I am Brahman, the supreme Reality' to the exclusion of all other thoughts. This practice ultimately enables one to root out the binding vāsanās at the deepest level and rediscover one's identity with the Self.

Hence, śravaṇam, mananam, and nididhyāsanam are the three steps that comprise the sādhanā of Advaita Vedānta. The Study Group is the forum for mananam. Nididhyāsanam, or meditation, is an individual practice that must form part of the daily sādhanā of a Study Group member. Some Study Groups include group meditation;

however, each individual needs also to find a time most appropriate for individual meditation.

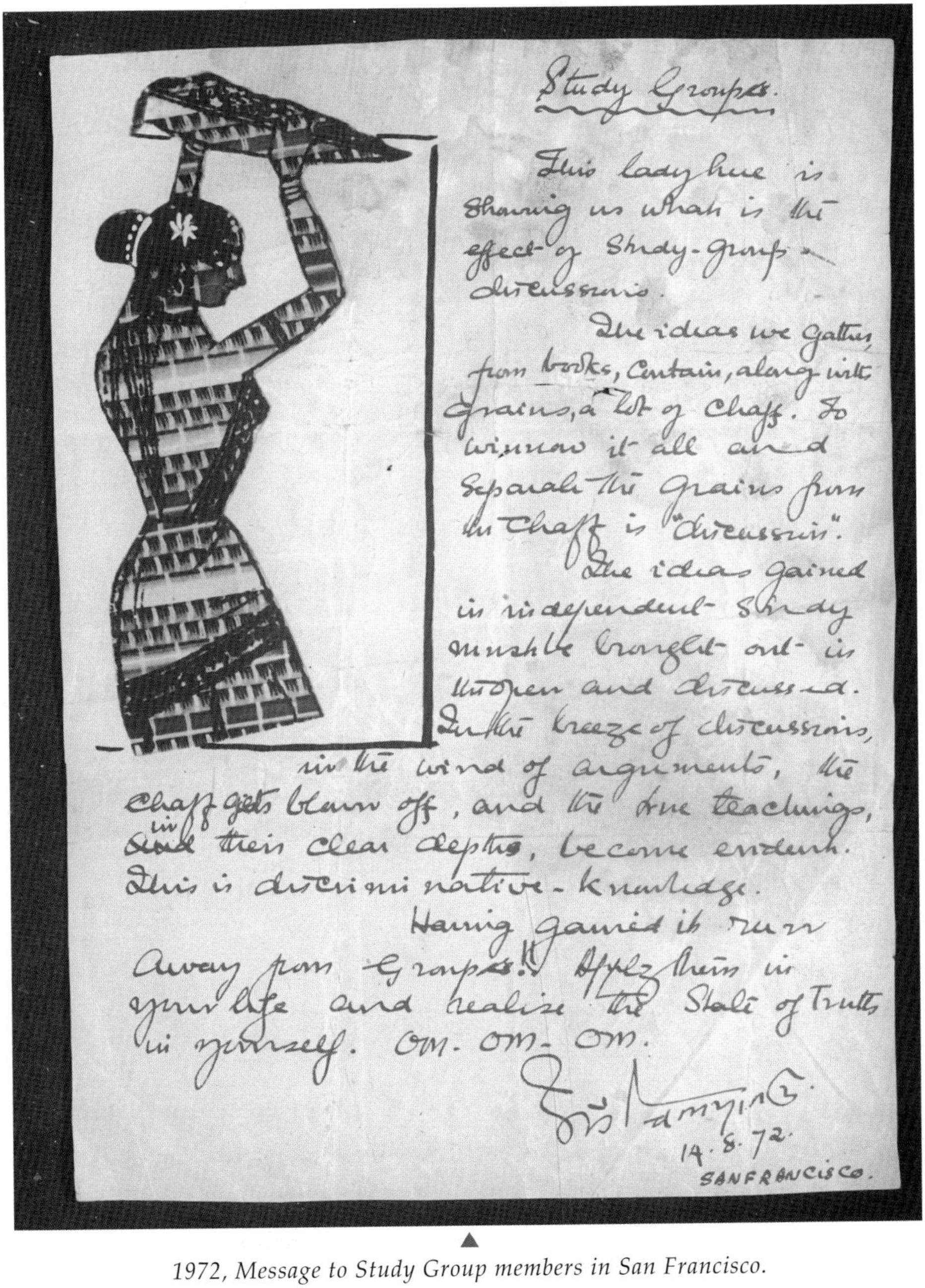

Study Groups.

This lady here is showing us what is the effect of Study-group-discussions.

The ideas we gather from books, contain, along with grains, a lot of chaff. To winnow it all and separate the grains from the chaff is "discussion".

The ideas gained in independent study must be brought out in the open and discussed. In the breeze of discussions, in the wind of arguments, the chaff gets blown off, and the true teachings, in their clear depths, become evident. This is discriminative-knowledge.

Having gained it run away from Groups!! Apply them in your life and realise the State of Truth in yourself. OM. OM. OM.

14.8.72.
SANFRANCISCO.

1972, Message to Study Group members in San Francisco.

In a few exceptional cases, śravaṇam alone can lead an individual to liberation. King Parīkṣita, the grandson of the Pāṇḍava Prince Arjuna of the *Mahābhārata*, gained liberation in just seven days merely by listening to the stories of the *Śrīmad Bhāgavatam*. That kind of listening implies a complete tuning to the Guru so that the latter's experiences echo in the heart of the student. However, few have that ability to listen with a pure, focused mind accompanied by a burning desire for the Ultimate. The vast majority, therefore, are unable to circumvent the following two stages of mananam and nididhyāsanam. It is for this majority that Gurudev instituted the Study Group.

The famous story of the churning of the ocean, a collective enterprise by the *devas* (gods) and *asuras* (demons), is symbolic of this process of purifying the mind. Both devas and asuras ardently seek the nectar of immortality which lies hidden under the milky ocean. The milky ocean signifies the mind and its hidden potential, which can be drawn out only through patient and sustained churning. The herbs and plants in the ocean represent the knowledge we gain through śravaṇam with a sāttvik mind. Thereafter, comes the hard work of churning. It takes time and requires patience and dedication. Even though each individual has to give his best, it is also a collective effort. Similarly, in the Study Group, mananam is continued during the week as an individual activity but, during the weekly class, it becomes a collective activity. With that mananam, we become fit for the third stage, nididhyāsanam, or meditation. That is when things begin to happen. According to the story, the poison comes out first and is swallowed by Lord Śiva who holds it in his neck; hence, the blue color of the neck and his name, Nīlakaṇṭha. Then come out the white elephant, the white horse, and other gifts of the ocean. Similarly, when the relatively quietened mind settles down for meditation, deep thoughts and inclinations buried in the subconscious rise to the surface. Many of these are negativities, which may shock the meditator. This is the poison from the depths of the mind that is surfacing and getting dispelled. As the meditation grows deeper, great treasures also surface. These are the gifts of the mind. They motivate and inspire one to continue on the journey.

The churning of the ocean. Based on a Persian translation of the Mahābhārata, *Murshidabad, Provincial Mughal, circa* A.D. *1800. Courtesy of the National Museum, New Delhi.*

This whole process implies self-effort, for the Guru can only point the way. His experience cannot become the disciple's experience. No one else can think and act for us. That is why at the end of the *Bhagavad-gītā* (XVIII.63), Śrī Kṛṣṇa tells Arjuna: "I have declared to you the most profound wisdom. Reflect upon it fully and act as you choose."

Strengthening faith and devotion is the second objective of the

Study Group. Without faith in the Self, in the teaching, and in the teacher, progress is impossible. Beliefs change but faith does not. In fact, belief transforms into faith when reinforced with conviction and clarity.

Blind faith is dangerous, for it is liable to be shaken by a strong personality or an untoward experience in life. We often see around us people who appear to be devout but who suddenly claim to have given up belief in God. Having gone through a bitter disappointment or tragedy, their faith in God and in the power of prayer gets shaken. In other words, their faith, in a time of crisis, proves to be conditional.

The Study Group, which encourages multiple views and counter-views on a given topic, is the platform for testing one's convictions. Constructive discussion on the subject invariably enables a reasoned faith to take root. Once doubts have been dispelled and clarity has been achieved, then alone is the individual free from confusions and uncertainties provoked by passing remarks, happenings, or advice from different quarters.

Being part of a Study Group enables a deep connection with the Guru through his commentaries and observations. Connecting with the Guru's words is creating the deeper and lasting ties with the Guru; for the Guru is not a person, he is the personification of knowledge and realization. He is that knowledge which enables one to reach deep within and find oneself; and it is that knowledge to which one must be completely devoted.

The process of spiritual unfoldment is a gradual one. As Gurudev describes:

> Study alone is not enough; there must be practice. Think of the great ideas constantly. Compare the way you have been living and the ideal you have. Feel ashamed of the disparity between the two. The courage and strength to live up to what you aspire to must come from within you. Nobody else can

do this for you. And to discover it, you need more and more study, discussion, and personal mental engagement in these ideas. Constantly, you have to expose your personality to this ethereal healthy atmosphere. Then your personality starts unfolding. As a result, you start expressing it now and then unconsciously. You feel good that you could withstand a little temptation or maintain your equanimity in the face of a tragedy that would have shaken you up earlier. Slowly you begin to glimpse the changes that have come about in yourself as a result of your study. These must gradually become a part of your personality, and then you can say, "Yes, I have gained from the Study Groups."

> Read/study attentively,
> Reflect deeply, and
> Practice slowly.
> Swami Chinmayananda

As ideas that are studied become deeply absorbed, the mind becomes increasingly integrated. Such a mind, says Gurudev, will reflect as "beautiful ideology, admirable self-control, and enviable self-discipline. Soon, a time will come when this discipline and beauty will become your inherent nature."

Spreading the knowledge is the third objective of the Study Group. As Gurudev said:

Mission members who have been studying for two years have gathered sufficient material. Whether you understand it or not, you must spread that knowledge. I tell you, if you start doing this, eighty percent of the people will start adoring you. When you start talking, you become convinced, and you can bring out those beauties in your life....

Gurudev asked members of the Study Group to reach out to the atheists, for as he said, "An atheist of today can become a theist of tomorrow, and, in a few weeks, he may even become a great devotee." He describes atheists as:

> …the very people who constitute the field for Chinmaya Mission to serve. They need our sympathy and all our understanding. … They are highly intellectual and truly independent thinkers. … The yajña session invites them; Study Groups serve them. Our Lesson Course helps those who do not find it convenient to attend the regular weekly Study Group sessions.

The rationale behind the transformation of atheists is that knowledge in a human being never remains the same. As Gurudev says, our ideas and opinions constantly change and complete reversal in thinking is not unknown. The biographies of many saints and sages around the world witness the truth of this miraculous phenomenon.

Spreading this knowledge serves a dual purpose, as is summed up by Guruji Swami Tejomayananda:

> You are only sharing what you know and deepening your own understanding in the preparation for such sharing. And what we must remember is that the goal is not proficiency of learning but expansion of consciousness, greater mental purity, and inner joy.

> Every Hindu holds a duty and responsibility to study, master, and communicate the sacred knowledge to the world, which is now thirsting for it.
>
> Swami Chinmayananda

Inculcating a spirit of love and service to humanity is the fourth objective of the Study Group. Gurudev always emphasized that study must go hand in hand with selfless service, and the platform for this service is the Mission center. However, for those who have very limited time, daily life itself is the platform in which to serve (the family, colleagues, the community, and so on) with an attitude of worship. As he said:

> ...Knowledge of the *śrutis* gained through sincere, daily reading and continuous reflection upon them, facilitates selfless and dedicated activity, which helps one to quiet the mind.... With a purified intellect alone can one understand the words of the scriptures and the instructions of the Guru. Otherwise, it will be merely some dry, unproductive book-knowledge. Such knowledge is like writing the word 'sugar' in more than one language on a piece of paper and licking it for gaining the experience of its sweetness.

Selfless service inspired by scriptural knowledge is distinct from that done simply out of goodwill and compassion. For, as Guruji points out:

> Giving food is sevā (service), but helping people earn their own livelihood is a greater sevā. And alongside, if you can help them lift their minds, then that is the highest sevā. All these are different levels of sevā. However, I think that the greatest service any person can do to this world is to bring about transformation within himself or herself. If he or she does that, everything will be fine. The problem is that we only seek to change others! So if you can change yourself, then you can give maximum happiness to the maximum number of people for the maximum time. This is our Mission statement. And when you live the vision of the Mission, that is, *look at your life as a whole and live a whole life*, then you will trigger an

inner transformation in yourself which will result in a happy world around you.

Only the individual whose vision rises above his individual ego and selfishness can serve the world. For, in that vision, the world and the individual are not separate from each other. Without spiritual knowledge, individuals tend to remain selfish and live only for their personal ends.

Fostering ties between members to create a sense of family is another objective of the Study Group. Over the years, such ties become so strong that they result in lifelong friendships. Members of the Study Group also become an important support group, sharing their deepest concerns with each other in the hope of getting clarity on how best to deal with challenges in a spiritual manner.

Gurudev urges members to constantly bear in mind certain salient points:

Allow all other members of the Study Group to criticize you — let each member always learn to point out imperfections, when noticed, in the others. You are all in the green room now. Help each other to dress well. Let your old nature be completely drowned in the new. May you be reborn to the higher, to better serve the world around you.

Developing communication skills is indispensable for a successful Study Group. This implies that discussions are held in an atmosphere of mutual respect and appreciation, along with a genuine collective sharing of points of view. The transformation from argument to genuine discussion happens as faith in the scriptures grows, for persons who have doubts are more prone to argument.

The art of listening is an indispensable skill in all spheres of life. In Gurudev's words: "We should listen with a critical, placid receptiveness to what we do not already know. And we should challenge the criticism of those things we do know by quietly turning our intellectual searchlight within."

Training workers for the Mission. The Study Group is a forum for developing the future leaders and workers of the Mission.

Some Study Group members choose to continue their study of Vedānta by joining the Vedānta course at Sandeepany Sadhanalaya in India. They invariably become pracārakas, carrying the message to others through discourses. Some remain householders and become teachers and facilitators in the different forums such as Bala Vihars, Yuva Kendra groups, Study Groups, and so on. Yet others choose to serve in different capacities in the numerous programs of the Mission.

As Guruji points out, it is only those who are firmly rooted in this knowledge who constitute the real strength of the Mission. That strength is not gauged by events that are attended by thousands of people. No doubt, the masses are important because they highlight the thirst for knowledge that is present in so many people. However, it is only the handful of people who are drawn to the Study Group and, thereby, to the knowledge, who become core members and who dedicate their lives to the work of Chinmaya Mission.

> If you are a real devotee of the Lord, you can do more service to the world than all the politicians put together.
>
> Swami Chinmayananda

VII

The Role of the Sevak[4]

The term 'sevak' signifies one who renders sevā, or service. Sevā has two aspects: the physical and the attitudinal. Conducting the Study Group is the physical aspect of sevā. It is sevā toward the cause of svādhyāya, or scriptural study. The attitude, or spirit, of sevā, however, is quite distinct. It is not limited to any one physical act, but reflects in all the thoughts, emotions, words, and deeds of an individual. In short, it is a way of life. A true spirit of sevā is one that is guided by genuine compassion, concern, and love. It is an attitude of giving not just of material goods but also of time, empathy, encouragement, or knowledge.

The spirit of sevā, too, reflects at two levels: the external and the internal.

External Aspect of the Spirit of Sevā: At the external level, the Study Group sevak must ensure:

- regularity of the class.
- punctuality in starting and concluding the class.
- appropriate physical and aesthetic preparations for the

[4] Transcribed from Guruji's talk at the Study Group Sevak Training Program held at Chinmaya Vibhooti, Kolwan, September 8–12, 2009.

class such as the altar, lighted lamp, and adequate seating arrangements in order to create a loving and welcoming atmosphere

- a well-articulated discipline and structure, such as: complete focus on the topic and avoidance of digression; one person speaking at a time without being interrupted, and so on. This must be clearly stipulated when the Study Group meets for the first time.

The sevak plays the following roles:

- *Moderator*, who ensures that the class does not become a teaching class but remains an interactive one.
- *Initiator*, who sets the ball rolling in the class, leading the opening prayer and recapitulating the earlier class very briefly.
- *Facilitator*, who stimulates thinking and gives an impetus to the group discussion. He or she ensures that each individual lesson concludes with an idea, and resumes the chain of thought in the next lesson, creating interest for what follows.
- *Motivator*, who ensures that any slackening of energy or interest is quickly addressed and interest rekindled. The sevak must ensure that her own level of enthusiasm remains unaffected since that impacts members of the group.
- *Accelerator*, who keeps up the tempo of the classes lest they drag and become boring. As people become familiar with the subject, the progress invariably becomes more rapid. The goal of completing the course inevitably inspires all to do regular study and progress through the recommended texts.
- *Achiever*, who accomplishes the mission.

All this implies considerable effort and self-discipline on the part of the sevak. It goes without saying that a Study Group sevak must have attended a Study Group and have, at least, studied some of the texts prescribed in the scheme of study. Moreover, the text under study must be very clear to the sevak. While the sevak is expected to dispel doubts of members of the group, there will always be occasions when he or she is unable to answer a question. In that case, the question should be noted down and referred to a senior person or an Ācārya, who is invited periodically to the Study Group.

The Internal Aspect of the Spirit of Sevā can be characterized by the three qualities of tamas, rajas, and sattva. A tāmasika attitude would be one of acting out of a sense of compulsion, without any interest or enthusiasm. In this case, quite evidently, the group will not last long. A rājasika attitude, on the other hand would be one of doing the task out of a sense of duty, since a commitment has been given, possibly, in a weak moment. So the attitude is brisk and businesslike, as is often the case of teachers in schools or colleges who have no option but to complete the syllabus.

The sāttvika attitude is one where sevā itself becomes a worship of the Lord. In fact, the term svādhyāya has several meanings. It is the study of the scriptures in general; it is a personal study of the scriptures; and, finally, it also implies an understanding of oneself through such study. Hence, the Study Group offers the sevak a wonderful opportunity to reflect on this knowledge.

When the sevak of the Study Group considers the sevā to be a worship of God, the whole process becomes an elevating experience. Reading the scripture, reflecting on it, and discussing it with people are all various forms of worship.

The *Bhagavad-gītā* (XVIII.26) gives the definition of the ideal *sevak*:

muktasaṅgo'nahaṁvādī dhṛtyutsāhasamanvitaḥ,
siddhyasiddhyonirvikāraḥ kartā sāttvika ucyate.

Translation: The one who is free from attachment, is non-egoistic, is endowed with resolve and enthusiasm, and is unperturbed in success or failure, is called good.

The ideal sevak is one who is free from attachments to the gross or subtle results of actions. Sometimes, we seek material, tangible objects as the result of our sevā. Or we seek the more subtle forms, such as appreciation, gratitude, or felicitations. The ideal sevak is free from egoism and arrogance. Endowed with great fortitude, patience, and enthusiasm, he or she remains equipoised in both success and failure.

As Gurudev says:

> The leaders who come forward to inspire their generation for their moral self-upliftment must themselves be morally strong, spiritually evolved, and ethically good. They must have endless patience, limitless love, inexhaustible cheer, and immeasurable goodness. To create these qualities in the chosen few we had started our groups. In some places, we have to report that the groups themselves were the shameful scenes of quarrels and fights, misunderstandings and mutual animosities. How sad we must feel about such outbursts of the animal in ourselves. But I have my consolation: the operating table cures often, but it also kills sometimes.[5]

In a Study Group, sometimes everyone is present; at other times, many are absent. Sometimes, people grasp the subject very well; at other times, not at all. Things always fluctuate. Sometimes, classes grow in number; at other times, they do not grow at all. The sevak must remain unperturbed through it all. What helps in the development of such an attitude is one's own spiritual sādhanā.

---

[5] Swami Chinmayananda, *As I Think*, pp. 11–12.

1980. The message remained consistently the same.

Our group leaders and members must carefully avoid becoming mere pedantic scholars or mere intellectual inquirers. ... The secret of giving this mysterious 'touch of life' to ideas lies in its practice; live morality before you talk of it. Practice meditation before you preach it. Taste goodness before you recommend it. Gain bliss before you offer it to others.[6]

Swami Chinmayananda

[6] Swami Chinmayananda, *As I Think, pp. 9–10.*

VIII

Spiritual Sādhanā of the Sevak[7]

Just as every sport requires a basic physical fitness regime in addition to specialized training for that specific sport, so also does spiritual life necessitate a daily spiritual practice, or sādhanā.

Ācārya Śaṅkara emphasizes that even mastery over all six schools of Hindu philosophy cannot bring about an evolutionary fulfillment. That state of spiritual development necessitates reflection, worship (upāsanā), and meditation. Therefore, while mere discussion in the Study Group is all right in the early stages, soon enough the need for some daily sādhanā begins to be felt. Even though this remains a personal and private practice, sincere seekers find that it takes the Study Group activity to a deeper and more profound level.

The daily sādhanā of a Study Group sevak has both an external and an internal aspect.

The External Aspect of Sādhanā

It is important that every Study Group sevak keep at least half an hour for personal sādhanā. This should include the three limbs described by

[7] Transcribed from Guruji Swami Tejomayananda's talk at the Study Group Sevak Training Program held at Chinmaya Vibhooti, Kolwan, September 8–12, 2009.

Ramana Maharshi: *pūjanaṁ japascintanaṁ kramāt* (*Upadeśa Sāra,* verse 4); a simple pūjā followed by japa of one, two, or three mālās. The mantra may be of an individual's choice. Thereafter, some reflection on a portion of any scriptural text is recommended.

Some people might enjoy pūjā with mūrtis (idols) and the ritual of bathing the mūrtis and so on. Others are satisfied with just the offering of a flower. These details are a personal choice, but a half-hour is a must for daily sādhanā. Samartha Ramdas Swami, the seventeenth-century saint from Maharashtra, offers practical advice on personal spiritual discipline. According to him, it is impractical to impose too many disciplines on oneself, for then they become difficult to sustain. This is especially so in the case of a householder with multiple demands on time. However, some sort of self-discipline is essential.

Therefore, one should work out a personal practice, which can be maintained even if frequent travel defines one's life. Ideally, it should be completed early in the morning before one is sucked into the daily routine. It should be as intrinsic to the daily routine as brushing the teeth, eating, and bathing. Spiritual strength is built day by day, year after year. Only then can one feel its effect on one's personality, particularly when one is buffeted about by the storms of life. Just as we require physical strength and fitness to do physical work, so also do we require spiritual strength to deal with life until the end of our days. Such spiritual strength does not come if sādhanā is done in fits and starts. It comes when one ensures that the day does not begin without completing that aspect of one's routine.

If, for some reason or the other, personal sādhanā is missed on a particular day, it must be made up later in the day or the next day. That is to say, one must devote double the time the next day. If not, the practice will slowly but surely begin to slide. Doing sādhanā in a mechanical function is better than not doing it. For in the very doing, a discipline is being established. As one persists, the emotions begin to undergo a change, and reverence for the practice and joy in it begins to develop.

The Internal Aspect of Sādhanā

This pertains to the attitude with which sādhanā is done. Just as service, or sevā, should be performed as an act of worship, so also is any spiritual practice just another expression of that worship. An important aspect of internal sādhanā is extreme alertness, that is, a constant awareness of what is happening around one as also in one's own mind. Above all, it is constant awareness of the presence of divine Grace in one's life. To remain aware of that also implies consciously guarding the mind from false attachments, arrogance, and selfishness. All these constitute the subtler, invisible aspect of sādhanā.

Constant self-awareness is vital if one wants to take charge of one's life. Often, when embarking on a journey, people remember God; but when they reach their destination, they forget Him. One should remember Him in the beginning, the middle, and the end. Similarly, one should keep the Divine in the mind at every moment through self-awareness. That is real sādhanā.

It is not possible to forcibly create a sense of love and devotion. But it is possible to enforce a discipline on oneself. And when a discipline is followed rigorously, then love and devotion also gradually happen. So, while one aspect of sādhanā has to be done with effort, the other aspect must simply be allowed to happen. It is like eating. One has to make the effort to eat but digestion happens on its own.

Such practice of internal sādhanā is important for every spiritual seeker, but especially so for the sevak leading a Study Group, for he or she must be able to inspire others. This is only possible if the sevak himself or herself is inspired.

IX

Scheme of Study and Format of the Class

The scheme of study that Gurudev prepared was designed to offer a graded and systematic introduction into what is literally an ocean of knowledge. The Indian scriptures are a vast and rich collection of texts. Diving into them without adequate preparation is like diving into the ocean without knowing how to swim.

Often, statements in the scriptures appear contradictory and we think that their authors had confused minds. In order to grasp the subtleties of the subject, one must proceed to study it in a systematic manner. Then alone can the study become meaningful and inspiring and lead to a transformative experience.

The foundational texts of Vedānta are the Upaniṣads, the *Bhagavad-gītā*, and the *Brahma sūtras*; together they are called the prasthānatraya. A meaningful study of these texts requires a subtle intellect; for the goal is not simply knowledge, it is wisdom.

Although all individuals have an intellect, they do not, necessarily, use it to promote their own wellbeing. Often, they use it for self-destruction or to harm others. From the scriptural standpoint, the intellect must lead to a sense of complete fulfillment. Self-realization — the culmination of the intellect in pure Consciousness — alone gives lasting fulfillment. Without this, no matter what we accomplish or achieve, there will always be a sense of incompleteness.

A subtle intellect is cultivated through prescribed and guided study, selfless service, and devotion. The prescribed study for the student of Vedānta begins with the introductory texts, or the prakaraṇa granthas, written by Ādi Śaṅkara. These texts enable the beginner to grasp certain basic tenets of Vedānta and master the terminology, which has its own subtle nuances.

Gurudev, however, introduced an even simpler text, *Kindle Life*, by way of initiation into the study of Vedānta. This was necessary because most Indians in the post-independence era (and this is the case even today) had not had any exposure to the philosophy of Vedānta, or to any other Indian philosophy for that matter. *Kindle Life* is a comprehensive, crisp, and profound introduction into some key concepts of Vedānta. It sparks off the churning of the mind through its deceptively simple and short chapters.

Once the basic ideas discussed in *Kindle Life* have been grasped, some texts of Ādi Śaṅkarācārya are introduced. Here the novice (often for the first time) begins the actual chanting or reading of Sanskrit verse or prose and reads the translation of individual words and phrases from Sanskrit to English. At the same time, the concepts already discovered in *Kindle Life* are presented in greater detail.

When one embarks on the path of knowledge and follows the prescribed readings, all questions get slowly answered. For this, however, a mere reading is not enough. Constant reflection on what has been read or heard is a must. Guruji Swami Tejomayananda recalls:

> I remember when I first met Gurudev; I was so eager to start the Vedānta course. Once, I asked him a question to which he gave me the response promptly. Thereafter, however, he said that I would not have to ask any further questions, because the śāstras were meant to answer all questions. He emphasized that all I needed was patience and regular study of the text being taught.

There is a clear and logical development of thought in the sequence of texts in the prescribed syllabus. Those that are purely technical in nature are followed by others that are more practical and which offer concepts that can be implemented in daily life. For example, *Manaḥ-śodhanam*, a composition by Guruji, follows after the very technical *Tattva Bodhaḥ*. *Manaḥ-śodhanam* literally means 'purification of mind,' and without the purification (stilling the agitations) of the mind, no significant headway can be made in scriptural study. Having understood the means for purifying the mind, one moves to the fifth text in the syllabus, *Ātma Bodhaḥ*. With greater purity of mind, one is in a better position to grasp the technical aspects of this text, which is similar to that of the earlier *Tattva Bodhaḥ*.

Once basic fundamentals have been grasped, the study of the four kinds of yoga — karma, bhakti, dhyāna, and jñāna yoga — are taken up. These differences are understood through a study of *Upadeśa Sāra* by Ramana Maharishi.

Thereafter comes a text to inspire devotion, *Nārada Bhakti Sūtra*. Often the intellect needs rest with some sort of refreshment. After the *Nārada Bhakti Sūtra*, the seeker is introduced to the essence of devotion and meditation in *Meditation and Life*. Only after all these preliminary texts are thoroughly digested does one proceed to the study of the *Bhagavad-gītā*.

The study of the *Gītā* alternates with that of the Upaniṣads. After every few chapters of the *Gītā*, an Upaniṣad is taken up. The reason for this is that the *Bhagavad-gītā* is the essence of the Upaniṣads. In fact, the Upaniṣads are described as the cows, whose milk is the *Gītā*. An understanding of the Upaniṣads facilitates an understanding of the *Gītā*, and vice versa. In this way, clarity in the subject keeps increasing. This study is interspersed with some short texts by Guruji Swami Tejomayananda: the *Jñānasārаḥ*, which deals with the essence of knowledge, and the *Dhyānasvarūpam*, which discusses the essence of meditation.

When one follows the prescribed course of study, over a period of time, a subtle shift in perspective begins to take place. A spontaneous reevaluation of one's life begins to happen and, by then, the thinking individual has discovered that there is something immensely worthwhile to be gained by regular attendance of the Study Group, as well as personal daily study. The topics and questions that are dealt with each time are relevant to every one of us. The fact that they were equally relevant in the ancient eras makes it all the more fascinating, for one recognizes that the human mind grapples with the same problems in all periods of time.

> Read, reflect, recollect, reproduce.
>
> Swami Chinmayananda

For those who complete the prescribed syllabus, there is a more advanced study course available. The texts for the Advanced Study Group are all very profound philosophical texts. The last in the series is the *Māṇḍūkya Upaniṣad.* Gurudev especially recommended that the *Māṇḍūkya* and its *Kārikā* be studied throughout life.

While following this scheme of study, there are certain other select readings that are prescribed for individual growth and reflection. All this information is listed in detail in the Appendix, which also includes a list of CDs and DVDs of talks by Gurudev on the *Bhagavad-gītā* and *Vivekacūḍāmaṇi.*

Listening to these DVDs offers a prolonged engagement in śravaṇam, or listening. Therefore, setting aside a realistic twenty minutes or half an hour each day makes it a feasible exercise.

Format of the Class

Ideally, the group should form a half circle facing the altar, with the photograph of the sevak's Iṣṭa devatā and the picture of Gurudev or that of the Chinmaya Guru-śiṣya-paramparā: Swami Tapovan Mahārāja, Gurudev, and Guruji. The sevak should sit close to the photographs but be part of the semicircle. The various stages of the class are:

(1) Chanting of *śānti pāṭha* (peace invocation), followed by the *Guru Stotram*.

(2) A brief summary of the portion covered in the previous class.

(3) Chanting of the śloka under study — sevak or someone else leads and others follow. Thereafter, all chant together.

(4) One person reads the meanings of the individual words, followed by the translation of the whole śloka. Every single word in the śloka must be understood. Often a word may have two or three different meanings. There must be complete clarity about the meaning in that specific context. Then the significance of the whole śloka must be understood. Questions arising from the reading of the śloka must be discussed.

(5) The next person then reads two paragraphs of the commentary, and, thereafter, sums up what he or she has understood from those paragraphs. Others add their insights.

(6) The class proceeds in this manner until the commentary on the first śloka is completed. Thereafter, either the sevak or a group member summarizes the essence of the verse and connects it with the previous verse. Care must be taken to ensure that the deeper significance of the words and expressions in the verse have been grasped and that all doubts are cleared before proceeding to the next śloka. Above all, what must be borne in mind is that the śloka is part of a chapter, and the chapter is part of a text.

The entire text has a central theme or message, and the development of thought and the central message of the text must be kept in mind throughout the study. Another important point is to see how the lessons from each śloka apply to everyday life, because the purpose of the study is not just knowledge but self-transformation.

(7) The discussion ends with a brief summary of the main ideas covered during that one session for purposes of reflection and subjective contemplation during the week.

(8) The class concludes with the *śānti pāṭha* and the Chinmaya Mission Pledge (also included in the Appendix).

Although this is the format recommended for the beginners' Study Group, there are, nevertheless, many variations. In some classes, reading the commentary of the text in class is completely bypassed as everyone does their homework and comes thoroughly prepared. The facilitator then leads the discussion by asking the key questions related to that chapter, or portion of text to be covered. Generating discussion is far more important than merely answering questions.

When Groups face the challenge of finding someone who is able, in terms of Vedāntic understanding, to facilitate the class and generate discussion, they often base their class discussion on a talk by Gurudev or Guruji in DVD format.

Christine Grimmer and David Buchholz from Australia have this to say about video classes:

In our experience over the years in Australia, three main dangers can arise when using videos of talks in Study Groups:

1. Some members will be tempted to not read or reflect on the verses in advance since they will hear them from the video.

2. Because Gurudev's teaching is so captivating and clear, the mind becomes quiet, or blank, or members may feel shy to offer questions before him.
3. For people often tired from busy work and home life, the temptation arises to passively follow the video commentary on the verses without thinking, and some groups end up just watching the video for the duration of the class.

Sidhbari, 1987. Gurudev with Christine Grimmer.

Two positive approaches to avoid these pitfalls have been tried here in Australia:

1. Discuss the verses before watching the video. Then view Gurudev's video commentary for clarification and inspiration in the last twenty-to-thirty minutes of the class.
2. View the video commentary for twenty minutes at the start. Take five minutes to individually write down key points that each person recalls, or a question that may arise. Share the points and discuss them for clarification.

A. L. Ananda of Singapore uses PowerPoint slides to guide the class. The invocations, prayers, main points for recapitulation, the śloka under study, concluding prayers, and the Chinmaya Mission Pledge are all projected on a screen. The Sanskrit word meanings with English translation and transliteration in roman script make the whole process

Sydney, 1995: Christine Grimmer with Study Group members (from L to R) Frank Bailey, Hemand Ghosh and Kirti Bhima Shah.

visually interesting. For those who are visual learners, this becomes a useful tool. As Professor Ananda says:

> This is a good way for those classes where the discussion is not that intense and where people are often absent. Those who travel on business often miss a class or two in a row, and it is a big challenge to sustain their interest and ensure that they continue to come to the class. The summary, point wise on PowerPoint, helps them to get a gist of all the previous discussions. Sometimes to make it interesting, I also show one or two short video clips from Gurudev's video discourse, only to highlight the salient points.

Several Study Group facilitators record the Study Group discussion and e-mail the audio file to all members. That helps those who were absent, and it helps those who wish to do a thorough revision or who seek to clarify a doubt. Ultimately, as with anything, if genuine value is being delivered, people will come to the Study Group and it will be sustained. Additionally, members will also be inspired to start their own Study Groups.

Implementation: A Brief History

X

Phase I — The Beginning

The five phases described in this section are not watertight, chronological developments. Rather, they are an attempt to show broadly some of the important landmarks in the evolution of the Study Group over the last sixty years. The chronology would naturally vary, as centers were established around the world at different periods of time. What is highlighted is the many creative ways in which Gurudev Swami Chinmayananda sought to encourage independent reflection and group discussion among his devotees and disciples. Despite the changing times and new developments as Chinmaya Mission grew and spread, the underlying message always remained the same: be proactive in your study and then share the knowledge with others.

The first Study Group had come about spontaneously, and it had been the genesis of Chinmaya Mission. Through the 1950s and early

1960s, on Gurudev's recommendation, like-minded, inspired people in different towns and cities came together to study the texts that they had heard at the jñāna yajña. To further strengthen and sustain the inspiration of these early groups, Gurudev introduced the monthly publication called *Usha* in September 1958. Among other things, *Usha* shared reports and displayed photographs of Study Groups and their activities. Through the publication, Gurudev voiced his expectations to the members of the group. A second publication, *Tyagi*, published articles on serious texts and Gurudev's commentaries on the *Bhagavad-gītā, Vivekacūḍāmaṇi*, and other texts. Thus, while one publication (*Tyagi*) provided material for study, the other (*Usha*) reported on the progress of study. Both *Usha* and *Tyagi* were merged with *Tapovan Prasad* in 1963 and 1965, respectively.

By the early 1960s, over one hundred Chinmaya Mission centers had sprung up across India. It was time, therefore, to focus on a

1953. Finalizing commentaries for publication as Yajña Prasad.

◀ *1959. Every moment was spent in serving the cause of knowledge.*

uniform structure for the Study Group. How this formal structure was developed in the early 1960s in Mumbai is captured in a report by P. G. Ananthanarayan (Uncle Mani) in *Tapovan Prasad*, April 1964:

> It was in December 1962, after the conclusion of the 108th Jñāna Yajña at Lloyds Reclamation Ground, that the first three Study Groups were inaugurated and blessed by Swamiji. These groups were conducted more or less as a pilot scheme intended to gauge the extent of interest among the public for systematic and sustained study of the scriptural texts. The enthusiasm displayed by the members was encouraging.

In July 1963, at the end of the discourses on *Ātma Bodhaḥ* at Worli, for which there was overwhelming response despite the inconvenience caused by the monsoon, invitation through pamphlets was extended to the public to join the Study Groups. Surprisingly enough, nearly 400 people responded, and 250 were able to attend the first few meetings when the aims and objectives of the Study Group were lucidly and convincingly explained by the Pradhan (Administrative Head) of Sandeepany Sadhanalaya, Śrī Parthasarathy. Thirteen groups were formed. This unexpected response posed certain initial problems, the most crucial of which was the paucity of trained group leaders. The first three pilot groups were being ably conducted by the Pradhan in addition to his duties at Sandeepany Sadhanalaya, but it was impossible for him to cater to the demands of sixteen groups. Yet, to meet the challenge posed by Bombay, he took upon himself the task of conducting seven classes in a week.

Regarding the rest of the groups in Bombay, as an emergency and experimental measure, some of the members of the initial groups, who had by then completed the first two books in the scheme of study, were organized into a new group and trained as group leaders. Through Swamiji's Grace and Śrī Parthasarathy's untiring efforts, these group leaders have endeavored to share their knowledge with other co-seekers. In this process of recapitulation, every one of them is gaining confidence in himself and a deeper insight into the scriptural texts. The Bombay experiment has proved to be a success. At present there are 16 groups with a membership of over 200.

Employees of all categories of business organizations in this industrial city, both from the public as well as the private sectors, can be found among the members. There are doctors,

> lawyers, engineers, professors, teachers, officers, and also those who are working in the railway, shipping, aviation, banking, insurance, oil companies, and so on. The cosmopolitan character of the city is reflected in the membership of these Study Groups.

The pioneers of the Study Group in Mumbai included P. G. Ananthanarayan, K. B. Shroff, Rasikbhai Kadakia, Ajitbhai Kapadia, Nalinbhai and Hamirbhai Vissangi, Arvindbhai Tarkas, Bansibhai Shah, Jamnadas Moorjani, G. H. Muni, and Srichand Krishnani. By 1965, there were 30 Study Groups in Mumbai, 12 in Calcutta, 12 in Jamshedpur, 10 in Delhi, 10 in Pune, 8 in Bangalore, 8 in Chennai, 7 in Nagpur, and 5 in Ahmedabad.

The enthusiasm and dedication of some early groups is best highlighted by the way in which they were conducted. Of the eight Study Groups that were functioning in Chennai, one group met every day of the week during lunch hour at the office of the Railways. Another met every day at the office of P. V. Parthasarathy, a trustee of the first Chinmaya Publication Trust.

Gurudev's Guidance to the Study Group

Gurudev tended to the early Study Groups as a gardener to his tender saplings. He would meet group leaders and members during his visits to the centers and personally answer their many queries. He kept a close tab on their progress and introduced many programs to ensure that seekers derived the maximum benefit in minimum time. The first was the setting up of an examination system. As he said:

> These examinations are held in our Vedic System, not in the present-day spirit of *breaking* the student, but they are conducted with a view to *making* the student. If, in case, a student unfortunately falls below the standards of Vedic

expectation, he is not condemned as hopeless forever, but the teacher's instructions would be to purify and enable the student and thereby lift him up to the highest standards of efficiency.

Swamiji Writes...

C. M. STUDY GROUPS TO NOTE

★ I intend holding written tests to the members of Study Groups of the Mission Centres all over India, on various books in our Study-Scheme they follow.

★ I request the Study Group leaders to inform the Editor, Tapovan Prasad, the books they have completed in their group-study.

★ Question papers will be sent to the Group Leaders in a sealed cover which will be opened by them in their respective groups in the presence of all group-members, just five minutes before the exam.

★ The dates of examination will be informed next month through these columns.

★ The Branch Secretaries are requested to inform the group-leaders and do the needful in this regard.

S. S., Bombay, Sd. Chinmayananda
23rd Dec., '64.

The results of such tests were published in *Tapovan Prasad*.

A second development in this early phase was the inauguration of the Devi Group in Chennai on November 2, 1958. Like the first Study Group, the first Devi Group was also a spontaneous activity. The initiative came from a woman devotee who organized a weekly meeting with a group of women to discuss the scriptures and to see how the knowledge gained from that could be applied to their

SWAMI CHINMAYANANDA
SANDEEPANY SADHANALAYA

Sakhi Vihar Road, Powai,
Bombay 70.

C. M. STUDY GROUP EXAM.—I: KINDLE LIFE
April 26, 1964.

Note: All the questions are to be answered.

Write legibly.

Hand over the answer paper to the Group Leader who in turn will give to the Secretary for despatch to the Editor, Tapovan Prasad

Give your name address, and also the name of the Group Leader.

TIME: 3 Hrs. *MARKS: 100*

Questions :

1. "True religion never dies: Hinduism is not dead". Discuss. 15
2. Compare in general the philosophy of the West to that of the East. 10
3. More often than not, experiences in life give us only degrees of satisfaction, not complete happiness. Explain briefly why? 15
4. "Hinduism is a universal religion." How will you justify this statement. 15
5. "All techniques of self-improvement must be at the outset directed towards the disciplining and strengthening of the intellectual and psychological entities in us." Why? 10
6. Explain briefly the rise and fall of man. 15
7. How does Japa help in one's spiritual evolution? 10
8. What relationship do you find between the contents and the title of the book? 10

specific domestic and family problems. When they informed Gurudev of this latest Chinmaya Mission activity, they received his blessings and encouragement. He named them the Chinmaya Devi Group. Devi Groups are regular Study Groups with perhaps a little more chanting included in the program than in other Study Groups.

1959. Chinmaya Devi Group, Kollengode, Kerala. Gurudev with the senior Rani of Kollengode to his left and Rani Radhika Devi Nambudiripad to his right.

Another important landmark of this phase was that Gurudev took some of the devoted Study Group sevaks with him to the different towns and cities where he was invited for jñāna yajña. After the yajña, they helped organize newcomers into Study Groups and Devi Groups. There was an obvious hunger for spiritual knowledge among all age groups. At the same time, some Study Group sevaks were encouraged to give discourses, offering further impetus to the growth of the Mission. In Kerala, Sri Pisharodi held jñāna yajñas in Malayalam, taking Gurudev's message into the interiors of his homeland. Other such members included C. J. Vasudevan in Chennai, Dwarakanath Reddy in Bengaluru, and P. G. Ananthanarayan (Uncle Mani) in Mumbai.

It was during this early period that the Chinmaya Mission Pledge was introduced for the first time by Gurudev himself. The occasion was the closing session of the two-day All India Chinmaya Mission Conference held in Chennai on July 19–20, 1964. One-hundred-and-forty delegates, observers, and other visitors who were present took the Pledge on that occasion.

Characteristics of the Early Study Group

The early Study Groups had certain marked characteristics. To begin with, several lasted for many years — easily eighteen to twenty-five years — and completed the entire prescribed syllabus.

EXCERPTS FROM LETTERS OF GURUDEV TO NALINBHAI VISSANGI, MUMBAI

OCTOBER 5, 1977 - ALLAHABAD

Brahmacharis (and Brahmacharinis) have all enjoyed their contact with the Study Group activities. It has been to them a revelation. They never suspected even a fraction of this behind the innocent looking Sandeepany!

They have made an elaborate report of their own — with probably their suggestions. I have not yet gone through it.

JULY 12, 1987 - ORLANDO, FLORIDA, U.S.A.

After 22 years of weekly satsang, you have completed study of all books. Great.

A second characteristic was that several members of the early Study Group became Swamis and Brahmacārīs. Natarajan Iyer became Swami Dayananda (no longer with the Mission), Kanti Iyer became

Swami Shanthananda, and Rangaswami Iyer's daughter became Swamini Pavitrananda (who passed away prematurely). The Study Group in Bengaluru produced Swami Haridasananda (no longer with the Mission) and Brahmacārī Nitya Chaitanya, who later became Swami Sukhbodhananda (no longer with the Mission and presently head of Prasanna Trust). Several others did the Vedānta course at Sandeepany, Mumbai. Although some did not remain with Chinmaya Mission, most have continued to teach and propagate Advaita Vedānta, thus fulfilling the vision of Pūjya Gurudev.

Finally, because of their dedicated study, Study Group sevaks came to be looked upon as role models. As the late Maheshchandra Rao of Mumbai recalled:

> Uncle Mani is a role model. He is an example of living Vedānta as taught by Gurudev. He and others, like K. B. Shroff, lived what they talked about. K. B. Shroff's class was like a military rule. If he said something, he did it. If he told you to do something, you did it because he was so rooted in values. His words, like that of Uncle Mani and others, carried weight because of their sādhanā and, because of that, they had Gurudev's Grace. They had absorbed Gurudev's vision and they converted all the others to His vision.

Swami Swatmananda had a perfect role model in his grandfather, Yashwant Tarkas:

> My grandfather would go regularly to conduct a Study Group. I have seen him going in rain, storm, or cyclone. Gurudev had said that, even if nobody comes, the sevak must go, light the lamp, chant the *Guru Stotram*, and come back. I saw my grandfather do just that. His dedication touched me deeply and I marveled at how Gurudev inspired him. Often, he went and there would be no class. So when I joined a CHYK class

Chennai 1960s. Sri Yashwant Tarkas and Smt. Meena Tarkas receiving Gurudev with Poorna Kumbha.

at the Mission center. I was regular, even when many were not. If nobody came, I would attend the evening arti [āratī, or worship] and come home. But I continued to go and kept my inner fire burning because I had seen my grandfather do that.

Chennai 1960s. Sri Yashwant Tarkas and Smt. Meena Tarkas with Gurudev.

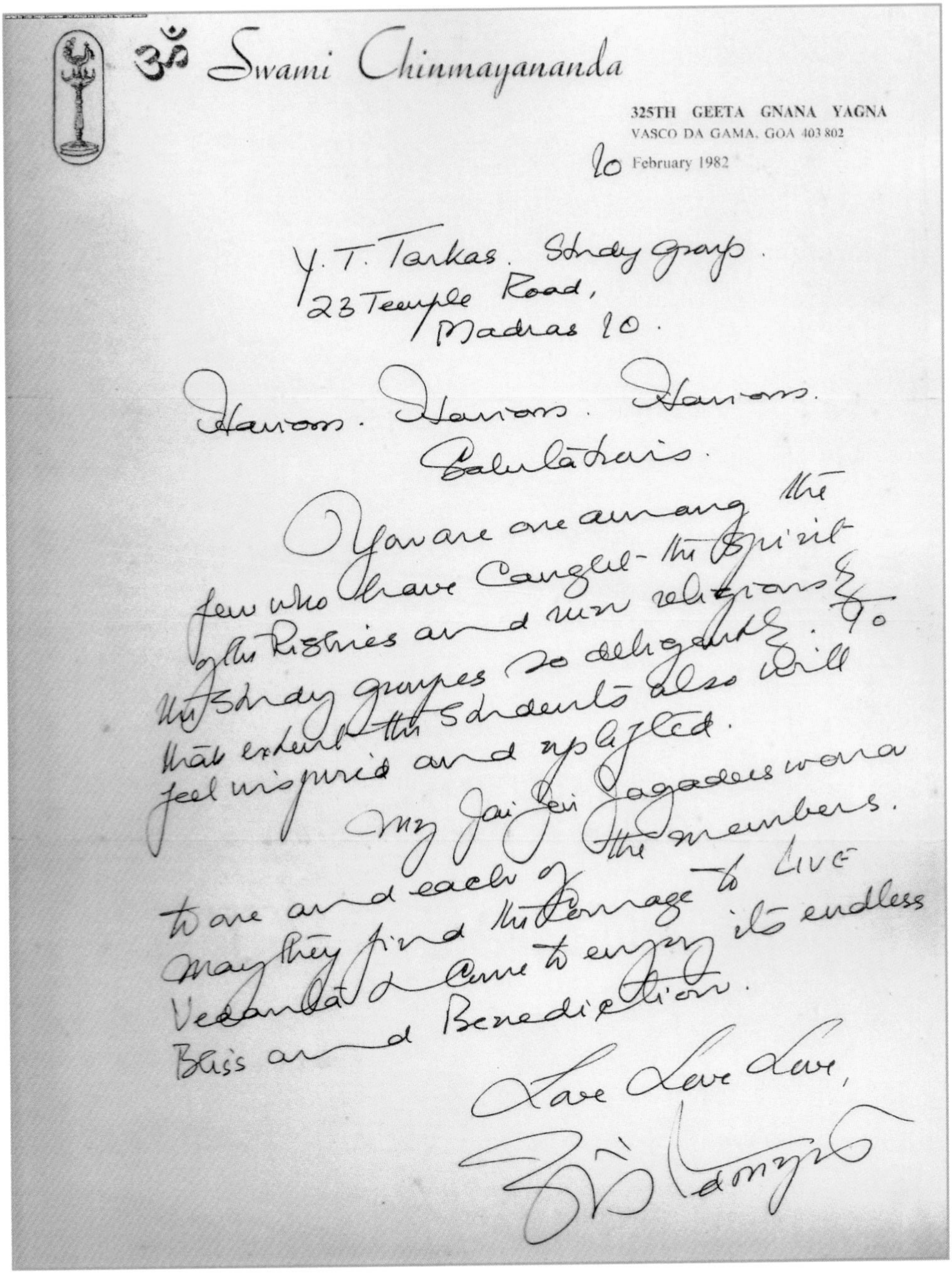

ॐ Swami Chinmayananda

325TH GEETA GNANA YAGNA
VASCO DA GAMA, GOA 403 802
20 February 1982

Y.T. Tarkas. Study group.
23 Temple Road,
Madras 20.

Harom. Harom. Harom.
Salutations.

You are one among the few who have caught the Spirit of the Rishies and run religious study groupes so diligently. To that extent the students also will feel inspired and uplifted.

My Jai Sri Jagadeeswara to one and each of the members. May they find the courage to LIVE Vedanta & come to enjoy its endless Bliss and Benediction.

Love Love Love,

[illegible]

EXTRACT FROM THE LETTER OF GURUDEV
TO Y. T. TARKAS

SEPTEMBER 27, 1978 - SIDHBARI

People like your good Self are the very corner stones of the Chinmaya Movement. It is people like you, all over the world, who silently work to prepare the field for Swamis and Brahmacharis to function.

▲
1968 Delhi Study Group Members: seated extreme left – Sheela Sharma, Shakuntala Bindra (in black sari). In front of Gurudev – Sheela Puri, Mrs. Jagdish Prasad and Janaki Naik. Standing, left – Ursula Zieschang, Jairam, Bharati Sukhatankar, Jagdish Prasad, P. K. Damayanti, and K. L. Kharbanda in white bush shirt. From the collection of Mrs. Sheela Sharma.

Swamiji Writes . . . .

MISSION CENTRES TO NOTE

July 29, 1963.

Dear Seekers,

Sivoham! Sivoham! Sivoham!
Salutations! !

Study classes are running well now in many of the Mission Branches. This is indeed quite satisfying.I must congratulate everyone of you for your ardent devotion to the cause and the steady perseverance in the pursuit. This will produce a new awakening in the midst of our National community.

The study classes are a serious assembly for intense study, it's a divine hall-of-study.

The scriptures were initially given out in an atmosphere of supreme devotion and reverence of the student, and admiration and joy of the teacher. We must learn to recapture this holy attitude in every study-class-session.

Hence I insisted that we must have an altar, and we must start our day's discussions after a little prayer and silent meditation.

As I watch over these sessions, I find that all of you start the studies in the right-attitude, but as the discussions warm up each one in his anxiety to "win a point" lose his balance and proportion. Thereafter the arguments run meandering into noisy streams eroding all understanding cultivated so far through scientific thinking.

This danger could never have happened when students in the past studied at the feet of their Master. Their reverence and faith in their Master served as revetments, between which thoughts ran straight to the goal. Today in our study-groups we miss this reverential attitude in our hearts. Hence the danger of the discussions ending in noisy confusion.

Develop an attitude of respect for the group leader. The group-leader while he is presiding over the study class is My Representative. He talks, no doubt, guided by his understanding; but he is watched over by me. You must see in him a distant shadow of Me. This will lend the necessary reins to the vanity of the human in each one of us.

The group-leader also must help the members to develop this love and affection to him, through his own beauty of life, self-development, true affection for all members under his charge, punctuality, study, and above all missionary sincerity. He must learn to admit his faults readily, must be ever willing to learn from the group discussion. With true and sincere love from the depths of your heart, you can win any heart.

I am sure, these instructions will be followed by all members and group-sevaks of study-groups all over India.

Sandeepany Sadhanalaya
Bombay

–Chinmayananda.

1980. Gurudev with Sheela Sharma, devoted Study Group Leader in Allahabad and Delhi.

XI

Phase II — Expansion and Consolidation

This phase is marked by the beginning of the Study Group outside India and by the introduction of creative new measures to further promote the activity in India.

The Study Group Abroad

In 1965, Gurudev Swami Chinmayananda visited thirty-nine cities in Southeast Asia, the U.S., Canada, the West Indies, Europe, and the Middle East. Similar Global tours followed in the successive years as Gurudev reached out to more and more people around the world. The interest sparked by these visits led to the establishment of the Study Group in several countries and, eventually, to the development of full-fledged Chinmaya Mission centers.

This genuine hunger for knowledge was apparent in the numbers that attended Gurudev's talks and his yajñas. In the U.S. and Europe, the audience was mostly American and European, respectively. In Asia, England, and the West Indies, it was largely made up of domiciled Indian communities.

Gurudev decided that the most appropriate form of study for a non-Indian audience would be a short, intense, time-bound program. That would not only provide a sound foundation for the sincere student, but it would also weed out those whose interest was superficial. Such a course would also be appropriate for those Indians who had grown up outside India.

Thus, the idea of a Postal Lesson Course took shape, and, by January 1967, the first lesson was on its way to the students. In 1971, when Gurudev undertook his longest tour of foreign countries for missionary activity, eight hundred people signed up for the Lesson Course.

Under this scheme, a course of twenty-four lessons in the fundamentals of Vedānta was to be sent through postal mail during the span of one year. Worksheets were to be answered every fortnight by the students and sent to India. These would be corrected and evaluated by specially appointed examiners and returned to the students. Missing even one lesson would result in the student being considered a dropout. Thereafter, if he or she wished to continue, it would mean restarting from Lesson One all over again. "In short," said Gurudev, "not only your steady effort but God's Grace, too, will be needed to finish the Course."

Those who successfully completed the course were awarded a certificate and urged to share the knowledge they gained with five others in the neighborhood. Wherever he was in the world, Gurudev personally responded promptly and meticulously to each query of the Lesson Course students. Many early Study Groups in the U.S. and elsewhere were started by those who had successfully completed the Postal Lesson Course. To make the Mission publications available to a Western audience, book distribution became an important activity and was first accomplished through the efforts of Nalini Browning and Leo Graves in Napa, California.

Beth Patterson, an American lady, started the first Study Group in San Francisco soon after Gurudev's first yajña there in 1966. Those who joined were mainly young Americans in their twenties, of which some were from the 'hippie' community. Other pioneers in the Study

Group activity in the Bay Area, California, were Nalini Browning in Napa, Rudite Emir in San Francisco, Luis Jaurengui in Oakland, and Uma Jeyarasasingam (now Ācārya) in South San Francisco.

San Francisco, 1968. Members of the first San Francisco Study Group: L to R – Nalini Browning, Beth Patterson, Rick Flinders, K. J. Jeyarasasingam, Carol and Tim Flinders, Uma Jeyarasasingam and daughter Gayathri.

In New York, P. V. Krishna Moorthy (now Ācārya) and David Robinson were the pioneers of the Study Group in Manhattan in 1970–71, Ram and Sheela Kirpalani in New City, the Bronx (1974), and Sharada Kumar (now Ācārya) in Long Island (1978). In Boston it was Gopal Sarma and Mimi Robins in 1971. In Washington, D.C., the first Study Groups were started in 1978 by Richard and Barbara Mullens, the parents of Vilasini Balakrishnan (now Ācārya), and by Joan Blanton Hart. In Flint, Michigan, Apparao Mukkamala took the initiative in 1978, while Vilasini Balakrishnan was the pioneer in Chicago in 1980.

In Canada, Charlotte Wallman organized the first Study Group in Toronto in 1973 shortly after Gurudev's first visit to the city. Barrie Dykes gave a new boost to Study Groups at the University of Toronto after he completed the Vedānta Course in Sandeepany Sadhanalaya, Mumbai, in 1978. Brahmacāriṇī Robyn (Robyn Thompson) played an active role in starting and conducting Study Groups in Vancouver.

Williamsburg, Virginia, 1980s. Gurudev with Barbara Mullens Moorman (mother of Ācārya Vilasini)

Simultaneously, the Study Group made an appearance in Kuwait (Chander Gurbaxani, 1970); Zurich, Switzerland (Krishnan Padiarth in 1977) and Manila (Kishu Gagoomal in 1979); Singapore (K. P. Daswani in 1986) and Muscat in 1984. Gradually, the activity spread to new cities and localities.

As in India, Gurudev empowered individuals to hold classes and spread the message of Vedānta in their communities. Luis Jaurengui was asked by Gurudev in 1975 to start holding *Gītā*- jñāna-yajñas in his native Spanish. Members of the Study Groups in the San Francisco Bay Area organized these first talk series.

New Programs for the Study Group in India

In the initial stages of the expansion of Mission activities overseas, Gurudev had less time for the centers in India. In November 1966, he sent the following message through *Tapovan Prasad* to his devotees:

> I would certainly love to see here that the Mission Branches are independently organizing symposiums on ethical, moral, and spiritual topics, inviting the local thinkers and discussing topics of serious concern, such as: "The Youth and the Modern Crises in the Country." Similarly, the Branches can invite well-known philosophers and authorities to give a basic study of Ramanuja, Madhwa, and Vallabhacharya — even Jain and Buddhistic ideas. These should complete the education of the members.

In every way, there was to be an expansion of knowledge. In addition to the study of scriptural texts, seekers of knowledge were to be exposed to the thoughts, writings, and talks of wise men from different spiritual traditions of the country as well as topics of contemporary concern. Thus, the dynamism of thought was to be sustained. Contact with great minds would stimulate fresh thinking, offer new perspectives, deepen the general awareness, and encourage interest in spiritual as well as social and cultural concerns.

Gurudev foresaw that the study and discussion of his books could quite easily descend into banal and mediocre reading and discussion. The depth of study and reflection had to be sustained by exposure to wisdom from various sources — to take that same understanding to a deeper level and to keep the mind ever agile and involved.

In 1969, Gurudev introduced, for the first time, the concept of vicāra yajña, or symposiums. Once a month, members were to gather together for one day and discuss a predetermined topic, the aim being to promote cooperative thinking. The first event was held at Mumbai, and the subject chosen was "Student Restlessness." This was also a way to motivate individuals to engage in social concerns for the wider good and apply Vedānta philosophy in national life. Vicāra yajñas for students, teachers, and principals were held in Chennai, Jamshedpur, Mumbai, Vishakapatnam, and several cities of Kerala.

EXCERPTS OF LETTERS FROM GURUDEV TO RUDITE EMIR, SAN FRANCISCO, CALIFORNIA, U.S.A.

DECEMBER 15, 1967 – COIMBATORE

The Study Course may be started with a program of listening to the tapes of the Swami, but it must seriously be taken up rigidly following the textbook *Kindle Life*. Study them seriously — some ten pages of it, so that at the end of the week, there will be 70 pages of material for discussion and mutual elucidation. Follow the books one by one as has been prescribed. You will be supremely benefitted.

JANUARY 14, 1972 – HONOLULU, HAWAII

To impart what you know to others and to prepare yourself to help them with their doubts would be beautiful, as your mind is held high in a state of joyous fullness. More than other members of the group the Study Group leader is benefitted by the study sessions.

FEBRUARY 22, 1972 – SANDEEPANY SADHANALAYA MUMBAI

Until the first three or four books are over from the Study Scheme, if you enter into the Gita or the Upanisads, you will not at all be benefited, and the students will have very many missing links in their chain of thoughts. That is why the Study Scheme has been put out. Total and complete satisfaction can be derived only when the student takes up the Postal Tuition [course] first. All may not realize this, and I cannot help them. After all, our work is only to advise. We do not want to advertise. In short, those whom the Lord inspires the right way alone can be helped on the spiritual path. In case there are students who have taken up the Postal Tuition, it will be very effective if you can organize one evening every week for them alone and strictly follow the Lesson Course scheme. At Powai [Sandeepany Sadhanalaya Mumbai], every student starts with this Lesson Course, and the rewards are stupendous. Hereafter, I would also put pressure because of the beautiful results seen. I must insist that all students go through the Postal Tuition.

MARCH 14, 1972 – TAPOVAN KUTI, UTTARKASI

The Study Group method has been found from time immemorial as effective — it adds a spirit to the sadhak in all his/her sadhana for the whole week. Be honest in your pursuit: be ready to "give" your ideas, as well as be tolerant and grateful to "take" other viewpoints. Consider them, and you have your full liberty to arrive at your own personal philosophy.

SEPTEMBER 27, 1972 – BROOKLYN, NEW YORK

The Lord must be infinitely happy about your work: 10 students for you! This is Grace! Let us be humble and, surrendering unto Him in devotion, act for His Glorification. A new surge of confidence, a new flow of wisdom shall stream into you, and through you to others. The more the surrender, the thicker this beam of wisdom-flood. Try! I am not exaggerating. It is our arrogant ego that clogs the streams of inspiration. Try! . . .

"New blood" cannot disturb the communion among the old members. Of course, they will try, but they will never succeed. In fact, through that contact you will find them being sucked into your communion! No doubt, a few of them may fail to discover this rapport — and they will leave. Your anxiety should be to guide those who are with you, and not worry over those who went away. They are the Lord's responsibility.

As Gurudev said, "We must learn to take up problem after problem — and there is no dearth of problems in our country — and learn to discuss it in a disciplined, reasoned manner, and with parliamentary precision and courtesy. Thus we can learn to coordinate all thoughts together."

Mumbai, 1969. Gurudev addressing participants at a vicāra yajña.

A second activity that Gurudev introduced to stimulate and enthuse Study Group leaders and members was the pārāyaṇa, or reading of the scriptures. Such reading to oneself or recitation of the scriptures in groups, Gurudev explained, forms a necessary routine for a seeker. It is called svādhyāya, or self-study.

In that 'marathon reading' program, a general view of the text is gained. Perhaps many portions may not be understood at all. But a general understanding of the theme of the text seeps imperceptibly into the reader. Gradually, other portions of the text are also clearly understood in the light of this general knowledge. Gurudev likened that perspective to that of a minister who, from a plane high above, gets a bird's eye view of the vast lands submerged in floods below.

Soon after the reading begins, a mood of integration between the reader and the audience develops through the technique of everyone silently and simultaneously following from a copy of the same book. Gurudev emphasized that one who understands can read well. What is read well is clearly understood by everyone in the audience. Regular reading aloud of some portions of the scriptures is important. Just as our mind constantly absorbs worldly information through regular exposure to newspapers and other media, so also can it imbibe spiritual knowledge at an ever-deepening level through regular pārāyaṇa.

A third development was that the Postal Lesson Course, which had originally been intended only for non-Indians, or Indians residing abroad, was extended to Study Group and Bala Vihar sevaks and sevikās in India. Eventually, as the Mission grew and more Brahmacārīs and Swamis became available to evaluate student responses to questions,

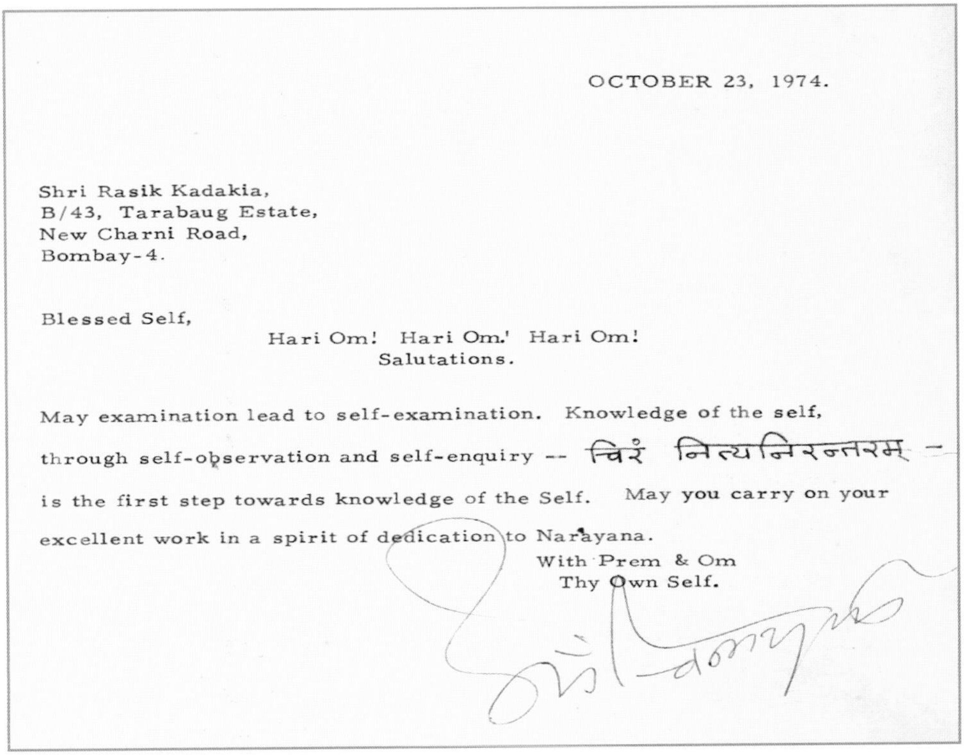

OCTOBER 23, 1974.

Shri Rasik Kadakia,
B/43, Tarabaug Estate,
New Charni Road,
Bombay-4.

Blessed Self,

Hari Om! Hari Om! Hari Om!
Salutations.

May examination lead to self-examination. Knowledge of the self, through self-observation and self-enquiry -- चिरं नित्यनिरन्तरम् - is the first step towards knowledge of the Self. May you carry on your excellent work in a spirit of dedication to Narayana.

With Prem & Om
Thy Own Self.

this program was thrown open to all Mission members, and, ultimately, to anyone desirous of such a distance study course.

Also, to this period belongs the establishment of the Chinmaya Yuva Kendra Study Group in 1976. Whereas, until 1976, interested youngsters simply joined Study Groups, thereafter, they had the option of joining groups specially organized for the youth.

Finally, as Gurudev's jñāna yajña was established as a seven or eight-day event, group discussions among participants during residential camps also became an established practice. This tradition continues even today.

Sidhbari, 1980. The Study Group of Sri Rasik Kadakia, with Brahmachari Vivek Chaitanya (now Swami Tejomayananda). L-R in first row – Kalavati Bhukhanwala, Vimla Merchant, Br. Vivek Chaitanya, Mr. Bhukhanwala, Rasik Kadakia, Murudheshwar. Second row L to R – Indira Joshi, Ajit Kapadia, Mr. Doshi, Dr. Joshi, Balubhai Kotak. This class completed the scheme of study and even today continues, although with many new members.

Sidhbari, 1983. Discussion Groups in the course of Gurudev's jñāna yajña.

Sidhbari, 1983. Seeking clarifications from the Master.

XII

Phase III — New Developments and Experiments

The third phase of growth saw two important developments: (1) Ācāryas were appointed to head the many Mission centers in India and abroad; and (2) Indian devotees from India started playing a growing role in the spread of the Study Group abroad.

Brahmacārīs Head Various Centers

From the 1970s, a growing number of centers were manned by a Brahmacārī or Brahmacāriṇī. With the arrival of the Ācāryas, Vijñāna Mandir classes, or the regular classes teaching scriptural literature to the householder devotees, became a new feature of Mission activity. Gurudev wanted those who underwent this training to involve themselves deeply in the various grassroots activities as their personal spiritual practice. In this way, he stressed, the knowledge would be kept alive in them through reflection, and that alone would help in the transformation of their personality.

On September 15, 1982, 375 students graduated from the Vijñāna Mandir, Mumbai, after three years of study under Brahmacārī Visuddha Chaitanya (no longer with the Mission). In his Convocation Address at the Jagadīśvara Temple, Gurudev declared:

> Mere study alone will not achieve the goal. Though erudite scholars and people doing research are available in plenty

▲
New Delhi, 1976. Vijñāna Mandir class in progress.

in our country, missionary work is what is required. The Sandeepanys and the CCMT were conceived for doing missionary work. If the students are to be made pundits, I would have remained in the Himalayas! Our objective is to unearth the Ṛṣīs who are buried under and make them walk again amidst us!

Mere study, without a readiness to work, is no guru-dakṣiṇā. Everyone who has studied must take a decision to become a Visuddha Chaitanya in society. If each one of you teaches two or three people, you will give life to the "dead Ṛṣīs."

Close your books and look around. There is corruption from top to bottom and people have become insensitive. Is this Hinduism? You want study and study — for what? Look around and see the insult and injustice! What are you going to realize? After thirty years of continuous roaring, people are becoming more serious. It is no use merely gathering the knowledge like a pundit and keeping it to yourself, as was done in the past. You can also go around screaming like them and become fanatics. So, study alone is not sufficient. The message of the Ṛṣīs must be communicated to every department of activity to suit the appropriate level of understanding — to children in the Bala Vihars, to teenagers, industrialists, and so on. All this needs independent reflection on what we have studied and overflowing love to convey [the message of Vedānta] to the people, backed by love and reverence for the Guru-paramparā. Take up the pracāra work in your locality through the existing channels of the Study Group, Yuva Kendra, Bala Vihar, and so on. Here is an opportunity to approach the untapped areas — tackling the old, the orthodox, and the scientific-minded in their own language. Śaṅkara has answered all — the 'Why' and 'How' and so on. Make your approach to pracāra very creative.

As a symbol of your readiness today, you will participate in a silent oath-taking ceremony by lighting a lamp and placing it in your locality on the map. Try your level best to spread the knowledge to others, *not* by mere words, but by the fragrance of your living, in your own actions. Spiritual values have a vitality of their own when it reaches the Heart. The Convocation is an occasion to declare your determination and decision to keep the goal in view and act — the real purpose and application of education.

If you expect Brahmacārī Visuddha alone to do it, it will take three generations! Light up other hearts or it will result in the burial of our culture. Let us not repeat the mistake committed by the present generation and hand it over to the children. Live and revitalize!

Where this objective of spreading the knowledge was taken seriously, the Study Group took root and has continued to flourish until today.

As K. G. B. Gupta, a senior sevak and former Secretary of Chinmaya Mission Bengaluru, recalls:

> Vijñāna Mandir classes in Bangalore were started around 1979 for the purpose of having an intense course, like in Sandeepany — two sessions in a day — to train *sevaks* for the mission and as Study Group sevaks, in particular. It ran for two years. It was conducted simultaneously at two places: at St. John's road and at Jai Nagar. The response was very good; there was a minimum of 20–25 people in each class and they would pay a monthly fee. It was a very rigorous program and exams would be held regularly. The majority of the Study Groups at present are from this course.

This rigorous training of *sevaks* in Bengaluru has ensured that there is a solid foundation for the Study Group in the city, and the activity has sustained itself over the years. It continues to remain strong until today and has become a part of the local Chinmaya Mission culture. This success is due to the dedicated training given to householders by the early Ācāryas; and it is also due to devoted and inspired sevaks who have been able to inspire seekers to join the Study Group all through these years and who have continued to empower Study Group members to start new groups. Above all, it is due to Swami Brahmananda, who has always encouraged and supported the activity.

In other centers, despite *vijñāna mandir* classes, Study Groups did not grow. Anjali Singh who attended such classes in Delhi has this to say:

> In 1976, I joined Vijñāna Mandir classes. They were held everyday and were quite intensive, single-pointed, and extremely good. In a way, we have done the whole Vedānta course. But there was one drawback. Because there were no Study Groups, we just listened. As a result, the *mananam* that

takes place in the Study Group never happened. Nor were we inclined to start Study Groups. Possibly this was because we were so used to just listening, that the confidence to lead such a group did not develop; or, perhaps, the inclination to do so was lacking.

The table below, based on information published in *Tapovan Prasad*, June 1982, gives an indication of the numbers that attended Vijñāna Mandir classes in different parts of the country, and the extent to which that translated into grassroots activity. These statistics pertain to only sixty centers in India since every center did not have the benefit of Vijñāna Mandir classes.

	1979	**1980**	**1981**
Vijñāna Mandir classes			A total of 2,152 people attended
Study Group (in 60 centers in India)	229 groups with total of 1,968 members	311 groups with 2,182 members	332 groups with 2,427 members
CHYK Study Group (in only 28 centers in India)	95 with total of 1,023 youth	110 groups with 1,292 youth	123 groups with a total of 1,447 youth
Bala Vihar (in only 48 centers in India)	339 with 4,277 children	377 with 5,696 children	417 with 7,169 children

If, according to the table above, 2,152 individuals had graduated from the various Vijñāna Mandir classes in 1981, then there was potential for that many Study Groups as each graduate was a qualified sevak. In fact, the number of groups, as we see, remains relatively small even though the number of Study Groups and Bala Vihars did grow from year to year. For Gurudev, knowledge without sevā was meaningless. This concern was voiced time and time again. In another message to his devotees in January 1982, Gurudev writes:

> Study yourself and teach others.
>
> If each one of you teaches two or three people, you will give life to the 'dead Ṛṣīs.'
>
> Swami Chinmayananda

We have some seventy dynamic brahmacārīs in the field and they are a very insignificant force, considering the emergency that is faced by the moral and ethical life of our nation. Therefore, I had been spending my energy preparing the white-clothed householders, initiating them into the texts of the scriptures and into the secrets of meditation. Thousands are practicing sincerely and hundreds are studying deeply, but very few have felt the need to spread the ideas among our people.

I have hopes that, in 1981, we shall find that many of our Chinmaya Mission Study Group members and vijñāna mandir students will come out in large numbers to serve the community with mini-yajñas. Each person may be addressing perhaps only 100–200 listeners, but when thousands are doing it, it becomes a great force.

Similarly, those of you who have the inclination and preparedness must visit schools and colleges and spread the ideas among the confused students. For this work, mainly the teenage workers must get ready. Teachers and professors who

> have been serious students of our books must come out with voluntary enthusiasm to explain the beauty of our culture, the duties of the individual, and the responsibility of youth. These would be the next programs of the Mission for creating The New India, well equipped to face all our political, economic, and social changes.

Besides Vijñāna Mandir classes, Gurudev also introduced a special six-week Pracharak Training Program for householders so that they could effectively supplement the work carried out by the Brahmacārīs. The first such program was held in 1991 at Sandeepany Sadhanalaya, Mumbai, by the Ācārya-in-charge, Brahmacārī Swarup Chaitanya, under Gurudev's guidance. This Pracharak Training Program has now become the Dharma Sevak Course conducted annually for six weeks at Coimbatore. It is also organized annually at Piercy, California. In 2012, such a course was held for the first time in Trinidad as well.

Indian Gṛhasthas Play a Growing Role Abroad

Outside India, the winds of change were blowing. As more and more Indians joined the Chinmaya Mission, the profile of Study Groups, particularly in the U.S., underwent a change. While the early members had been entirely or predominantly Westerners or Eurasians, they now became increasingly Indian. Indians joining the Mission and forming more Study Groups had long-term implications. Whereas for the larger number of foreigners, Vedānta was a serious commitment or a serious curiosity, for most Indians it represented a spiritual and cultural heritage that they felt proud to discover. Whereas for most Westerners it was a personal engagement, as far as the Indian population was concerned, it became more of a family engagement. That is why Study Groups and Bala Vihars grew simultaneously. Whereas initially the Study Group comprised the most prolific Mission activity, the Bala Vihar eventually became the most successful grassroots activity. The

Bala Vihar is virtually one hundred percent Indian, and it is the most popular activity of Chinmaya Mission in all the countries abroad where Indian communities are settled.

In Australia, Dr. K. T. Ganapathy, on advice from Gurudev, moved from Mumbai to Melbourne and started the Mission center there in 1981. She promoted satellite centers in Sydney, Perth, and Brisbane, and gave an impetus to the Study Group and other grassroots activities. The appointment of a dedicated Indian sevak was useful for drawing large numbers of the Indian community to Chinmaya mission.

Melbourne, 1994. Dr. K. T. Ganapathy first CM Ācārya for Melbourne, with Study Group members Bella Wong (front) and Christine Grimmer (back).

Manisha Khemlani joined the University of Sydney for a Master's degree in January 1992. Besides attending a Study Group at the home of a Mission member, she also started a Study Group with her Chinese and Thai flatmates, as there was no physical Mission center in the city. Shortly thereafter, she also started a CHYK Study Group. As she says:

> I started the CHYK Study Group with one of the Sydney youngsters who had tried to do so in the past. We arranged a get-together for young people, because by then Swami Swaroopanandaji and Guruji had already visited the city and held yajñas. So there was a group of people who showed interest. We had a couple of informal sessions and then we started CHYK with a bang. There was a proper study class. As the coordinator, I would ensure that there was always a lot of discussion. Although people in that group have now graduated and become parents, the tradition of CHYK continues.

Through all these developments, although Gurudev's emphasis on the importance of the Study Group remained constant, increasingly he gave the freedom to people to innovate new means of promoting the activity. The key point, however, remained that of reaching out to new people. In May 1978 when the Chennai Mission celebrated its silver jubilee, Gurudev sent the following message:

> Mission members, wherever they are, in whatever condition, their life's work is to discuss and impart the essence of Vedānta and to inspire others to live the dynamic, courageous, chaste life of love and dedication.

Be yourself a Sandeepany, one who lights the 'Lamp of Truth' in the hearts of all.

Swami Chinmayananda

In yet another message to members, through the monthly magazine *Tapovan Prasad*, he said:

> Till now, all of you have been fed by the Mission, and very many of you have consumed and digested much of it. It is now time that you start giving out to others what you have imbibed. It is a sacred duty. Our Upaniṣad Ṛṣīs insist upon it.

No other organization in India can accomplish this... You alone can do it. You are all products of my thirty years of tapas. Its total fulfillment can be only through your effort and your sacrifice of time and energy.

You all must consider this as your grateful Gurudakṣiṇā to the Upaniṣad Ṛṣīs and the Gītācārya. By their Grace, may you come to experience every year as a gift, and every moment a bonus.

EXCERPTS FROM LETTERS OF GURUDEV TO DR. K. T. GANAPATHY, MELBOURNE

MAY 31, 1987 – HONG KONG

To read, study, practice, and spread the ideas to others together constitute a Maha Adhyatmic Yajna and you have been doing this for years now at S. Pole!! How the Lord chooses His workers and pours through them blessings for others! In each of our visits, we vividly saw the growing effect of your continuous work!!

Look after your health. As a precious instrument for Him to play through, you have NOW a more sacred duty to maintain His vehicle in spick and span condition.

MAY 21, 1989 — BANGKOK

Learn to surrender to His will and act. We can't take the responsibility of taking the knowledge to everyone. We sing as best as we know. It is then His job to bring His listeners. Stop worrying — leave it all for Him to worry.

XIII

Phase IV — A Temporary Lull

This is a period, from the late 1980s and into the first decade of the twenty-first century, when in many centers in India and abroad, there seemingly occurred a marked decline in enthusiasm for the Study Group. It is not that the Study Groups stopped running. The older ones continued and, in fact, several seasoned sevaks even increased the number of groups they were leading. Several classes were also being held in the various regional languages. Despite this, the number of new people involved in the activity did not grow significantly.

Another challenge was that very few people were interested in starting a Study Group unless they had a certain minimum number of people. That minimum of five or six was not always reached, and so the initiative was never taken.

Jñāna yajñas were being held regularly in numerous places. The easy availability of books, audio- and video-cassettes, not only of Gurudev Swami Chinmayananda's talks but of other spiritual masters as well, made spiritual knowledge increasingly accessible to a larger number of people. The role of the Study Group was easily forgotten.

Gurudev did not mince his words:

> The yajñas are becoming a mere shell. The essential core is empty of any conscious creative pulsation. A Yajña Committee

selects a venue, advertises, gathers a crowd; and a Swami or a Brahmacārī exhaustively discourses upon a chapter of the *Gītā* or an Upaniṣad; the sincere listener intelligently gathers the information, religiously purchases a copy of the book, congratulates himself, and returns home. Generally, his sole preoccupation thereafter is to wait for the next yajña.

In almost every town in the country, we have successfully created a large number of automatons who regularly attend, gather the information and books, diligently pay the gurudakṣiṇā, collect the yajña prasāda booklet, and return home.

But the question is: How much of what you have heard has been digested and assimilated to become part and parcel of your intellectual personality? Do these ideas add a new glow to your performance in life? Have they opened up a fountain of dynamism watering all your activities in life?

From the very beginning of my yajña sessions in Poona, I have been repeating the same warning that your listening in large numbers will not an add an inch to my stature, nor an iota to the glory of Chinmaya Mission. The Mission's purpose is not to create spiritual parrots repeating our scriptures or the ideas contained in the Ṛṣī declarations. Our purpose and goal is to add an extra dimension to the Hindu community, exhibited in the beauty of their social and cultural activities. In this, we have nothing to congratulate ourselves....

...I will not have more chances to repeat my call to you to join Study Groups and organize your own discussion groups. The earlier my community realizes the importance of this, the easier it shall be for the nation to feel proud of her ancient heritage.

That brahmacārīs were expected to be equally creative in promoting the Study Group is clearly spelled out in the following message by Gurudev in January 1989:

SWAMI CHINMAYANANDA

TO ALL BRAHMACĀRINS IN THE CHINMAYA FAMILY

Blessed Self: Hari Om! Hari Om!! Hari Om!!! Salutations!

There is probably some confusion about the role of our Brahmacārins in the field.

First of all, they should remember that they are there to serve the community. And this they can very well do by encouraging, motivating activities at the grassroots level. Study Groups, Bala Vihars, Devi Groups, etc., are time-tested activities, which need to be initiated where they are not there already. Brahmacārins should start such activities and give them a lead, as sevaks.

We are no more interested in Vijñāna Mandirs. These schemes to teach Vedānta in detail, over extended periods, have not proved to be adequately effective. Study Groups could do much more than these.

Special camps to empower the youth to initiate and sustain grassroots activities became important. It was not just empowerment of youth by giving them an exposure to the knowledge and contact with other like-minded youth. The emphasis was clearly on how to promote grassroots activity so that these would reach an ever-expanding circle in the wider society.

The following report in *Tapovan Prasad* of September 1989 captures the spirit of such a CHYK camp at Kasargod, Kerala:

> A three-day Sevak-orientation Camp for Kerala CHYKs was held at the Kerala Sandeepany, Kasargod, under the guidance of H.H. Swami Bodhanandaji on June 23, 24, and 25, 1989.

> The purpose of the camp was to train CHYKs to conduct Study Groups. Swami Bodhanandaji conducted classes on *Self-Unfoldment*. Brahmacārī Ashish Chaitanya and Śrī M. K. Ramakrishnan conducted classes on important ślokas and mantras with meanings.... At the end of the camp, a written test was conducted and the winners were awarded prizes. Swamiji gave a motto: BE AN IDEAL CHYK BY TEACHING 10 CHYKs FOR 52 WEEKS.

Reasons for the Decline of the Study Group

An important reason for the decline of the Study Group is that with numerous centers growing, a variety of other tasks became necessary, requiring a greater number of sevaks. Celebration of festivals, pūjās, publications, the Ācārya's classes, and other programs in different parts of the city created the need for publicity, infrastructure, fundraising activities, administration, and so on. Ācāryas had to increasingly manage schools, reach out to a wider community, and engage in several new projects of the Mission whenever they were launched.

Young brahmacārīs who came fresh from the Vedānta course and who themselves had never been part of the Study Group failed to really appreciate the power of this activity even though in theory they knew all about it. Thus, they did not always go out of their way to promote it among new Mission members. At other times, despite their efforts, there was a resistance on the part of members themselves to start the activity. The passive way of simply listening to talks was always much easier and more comfortable.

Over the years, Mission projects have grown to include education, rural development, cultural activities, health care, old-age homes, youth programs, temples, and many other social-cultural projects. Innumerable men and women are engaged in these different areas of service. Several people feel that as long as they attend some jñāna yajñas or some regular classes, it is enough. They fail to understand the benefits of the Study Group. For those who do start new groups, the poor quality of discussion is sometimes the reason for people to slowly drop out.

Another major challenge has been the lack of trained Study Group leaders. Training does not necessarily imply formal training, because the early Study Groups were all started by those who had been highly inspired by Gurudev's jñāna yajñas and who did regular study and sādhanā. Likewise, today those individuals who are inspired by Guruji or the local Ācārya and who have attended a sufficient number of classes/yajñas and who are committed to regular study can become competent sevaks. At most, a short training workshop should be sufficient to equip them with the wherewithal to be effective Study Group leaders. Ultimately, it is devotion and commitment that make for success. When there is love for a subject, there is enthusiasm. And enthusiasm is infectious. Therefore, when individuals are thoroughly convinced about the power of this knowledge and its potential for self-transformation, they are fit to become Study Group leaders. Another quality of a dedicated sevak is the willingness to sacrifice personal time and comfort in order to conduct a Study Group.

Another *perceived* challenge is that the younger generation wants quick solutions and instant formulas. This is the justification given for a lack of people in the age group of 25–50 years in the Study Group. It is also said that there are plenty of takers for the yajña, precisely because it offers knowledge of a text in a short period of time. There is, in addition, the notion that one can learn a text from an Ācārya in a few days as opposed to the Study Group, where the process takes months. The fact is that the process of *mananam* cannot be hurried or compressed. It takes its time depending on the quality of the mind engaged in it. Learning a text in a few days is, at most, a superficial exposure to the text. Therefore, the Study Group will always remain an important phase in a seeker's life.

Many Study Groups come to an end because they do not follow the syllabus and go straight into the scriptural texts such as the *Bhagavad-gītā* or the Upaniṣads. Without a sound grasp of the fundamentals of Vedānta and all their nuances, real understanding does not come about, and the joy of learning fades. Conviction only comes from clarity, and clarity only comes when one follows a well-chartered and time-tested procedure for studying the scriptures. Those who have not followed the syllabus have often found it difficult to grasp the subtle concepts. Sometimes, people have lost interest and the group has slowly faded away. In some cases, after completing a text, a group has found that the understanding gained has been quite superficial, and so they have taken up the study of the same text again.

All these factors notwithstanding, the lull in the Study Group activity is but a temporary phase. It was perhaps Gurudev's way of letting seekers discover for themselves the wisdom of his words and feel the need to engage in the Study Group with fresh enthusiasm. It was no doubt necessary for a new inspiration to be born and for a resurgence to take place. That renaissance of the Study Group belongs to Phase V.

EXTRACT FROM LETTER OF GURUDEV TO DR. BHARAT NAIK, U.S.A.

JULY 12, 1993 - KRISHNALAYA, PIERCY, CALIFORNIA

As a Study Group sevak you must insist whenever chance comes to emphasize how Vedānta Study is empty if we don't try to live its values.

ॐ

Bangkok.
Thailand.
18. April 1990

Swami
Sandeepanji.
Hari Om! Salutations!

Get ready to reach
Singapore by May 22 to take
Ramayan in English
during Camp afternoons.
The Camp is May 22-29.
On 30th you can fly to
Bangkok. Be here some 15 days.
Take Ramayan evening.
In forenoon meet Ladies &
afternoon BV: Talks 7-8.30 PM.
Organise BV, D. Grp, S. classes &
CHYKs. Train the Trainers (leaders).

Coordinate with Ramesh
Daswani. Finalise it with him.

Love, Chinmaya

M
23/4

ॐ Trivandrum
15 Feb 1971

Swami Chinmayananda

Smt Padma Gupta,
S-156, Panchasheel Park
New Delhi 110017

Hari Om! Hari Om!
Hari Om!
Salutations!

You are requested &
Sincere in your study-classes
along with Prarthana Baran.
Sincere study, with
a pure heart cannot be a
mere intellectual entertainment
but this very study-session
can become a deep meditation.
Note and clear and
understand both learn to
seek and search with your
mind this depths essence
is yourself.

Love, Chinmayananda

XIV

Phase V — A New Dawn

This is the phase when technological developments have made spiritual study available to anyone who seeks it. It is the age of E-Vedānta, the E-*Gītā*, on-line discussion forums, DVDs, and YouTube. At the same time, a variety of in-depth training programs for the conducting of grassroots activity, such as the Dharma Sevak Course and the Yuva Veer Course, have met with remarkable success.

The Study Group is now possible over Skype or Google Hangout. So location does not matter anymore. In the U.S., free digital teleconference allows several people to have weekly discussions over the telephone as well. Ācārya Sharada Kumar of Ann Arbor, Michigan, for example, holds a Study Group over Skype for seekers in Kansas City. In Delhi, a Study Group led by Bhaskar Raman is held over Skype with participants from Pune, Mumbai, Chennai, Bengaluru, and some places in the U.S.

Some Growing Trends

In the early years, members of the Study Group took the initiative to start Bala Vihars. Today, it is often thanks to the Bala Vihar that the Study Group is able to recruit new members. In several cities, these two activities remain closely associated. In centers such as Chicago or Dallas, for example, the Study Group is held at the Mission center simultaneously with the Bala Vihar over the weekend. Every year when new children sign up for the Bala Vihar, their parents are encouraged to join the Study Group. Since there are several sessions of Bala Vihar on Saturday and Sunday, a considerable number of children and parents are involved in these two activities.

Another source of recruitment for new Study Group members is the vast pool of Bala Vihar teachers. Ācārya Sharada Kumar and Lakshmi Sukumar of San Diego have made it compulsory for all Bala Vihar teachers to attend a weekly Study Group to ensure that their own knowledge and spiritual practices are not neglected.

◀ *Sidhbari, 1992. Gurudev with Ācārya Sharada Kumar. At the back, Swami Subodhananda (L) and Swami Chidananda (no longer with the Mission).*

Dallas, 1992. ▶ *Guruji with Lakshmi Sukumar.*

Some of the young Ācāryas are playing a considerable role in giving a new impetus to this activity. Ācārya Vivek Gupta (Niagara Falls, Canada) who completed the Vedānta course in Mumbai in September 2007, has recruited many young and middle-aged seekers in the U.S. and Canada into Study Groups, which are steadily growing. The professional backgrounds of the members of Ācārya Vivek's classes are varied — entrepreneurs, engineers, physicians — and so is the age group, ranging from thirty to sixty years. The sheer numbers belie the argument that the modern pace of life is a reason for the decline in the number of Study Groups.

In Ācārya Sharada Kumar's experience, the numbers of those wanting to join the Study Group is continuously growing. This is perhaps due to a strategy that she has adopted to promote this activity. She has made it mandatory for parents of Bala Vihar children to listen to her weekly one-hour discourse on the *Bhagavad-gītā*. This is also the case in Chinmaya Mission Houston, where all parents and teachers attend the satsaṅga of Ācārya Gaurang Nanavaty every Sunday. Because the *Gītā* cannot be deeply understood without some knowledge of the fundamentals of Vedānta, those with questions and doubts are urged to join the Study Group, which is recommended as the forum where all doubts can be cleared in a small group.

In some places, the motivation to promote the Study Group comes through Guruji's insistence to a center that he will visit only if he sees some growth in grassroots activity. In Ahmedabad, Brahmacārī Atharvana Chaitanya narrates about what happened when his committee sent a request to Guruji for dates for a jñāna yajña:

> Guruji replied that he would consider coming in 2013 only if Ahmedabad, as a center, shows some progress in 2012. This was needed to shake people up. I took the opportunity to emphasize to members the meaning of progress. It implies a very strong foundation of grassroots activities. That is the

reason for the target of having fifteen Study Groups by 2015.

In Ghaziabad (a satellite town of Delhi), Brahmacāriṇī Pranati, organizes small yajñas (20–25 people) in individual homes. This is done as a buildup toward an auspicious occasion such as a birthday or wedding anniversary. The purpose is to inspire a small intimate group of family and friends of the host to start a Study Group.

Swamini Supriyananda does important spadework in the Bala Vihar, Hong Kong, cultivating in the young generation a taste for group study. As she says:

> From the time the children turn eleven or twelve, I introduce discussion into the Bala Vihar classes. The discussion is with the teacher. When they get to fourteen or fifteen years, I introduce short break-away sessions where they discuss among themselves and then come back to the bigger group and report to the teacher. They present their conclusions and the teacher discusses these with the wider group. I do this so that the children get a taste of learning through group discussion. And if they enjoy it and it suits them, they will, hopefully, participate in it later in their lives and maybe even start Study Groups.

Cross-fertilization of Ideas

As lifestyles in India and elsewhere face similar challenges, ideas that have worked in one part of the globe are readily tried out in others. This cross-fertilization of ideas has been greatly facilitated by modern technology and by a number of international camps.

As Youth Group Leader Milan Samani says:

> I started taking a Study Group in 2002 in London. At the time, CHYK was quite small in the U.K., and there was just one Study Group running. Prior to that, every year, Swami

> Swaroopananda would come in September and a Study Group would start. By December, the inspiration would fizzle out and the Study Group would slowly fall apart — until Swamiji's next visit.
>
> A few of us, inspired by CHYK Australia, took on the responsibility of building a proper CHYK class. We started small (three people in the class) but were disciplined in our preparation, and the class slowly grew. After the following camp, we suddenly had thirty people. We quickly aimed to start one new CHYK class every year. Currently, we have six classes, with an average weekly attendance of seventy. Most are young professionals aged 25–35 years.

The process of cross-fertilization of ideas has also led to the concept of Sunday School, which has been prevalent in the U.S. and other countries, to take root in India. It is a concept that implies a comprehensive engagement of the whole family on Sunday morning at one venue, usually the Mission center, where Bala Vihar, CHYK Study Group, and the adult Study Group are all held simultaneously. The concept was introduced in Mumbai in 2000 by Swami Ishwarananda and, increasingly, it is being followed in several centers in India and abroad.

The Role of Senior Sevaks Worldwide

Several senior citizens who have been pioneers of the Study Group activity for several decades continue to be stalwarts of the activity even today. The Study Group remains central to their lives, and many among them lead or attend multiple groups, thereby engaging in constant *mananam*.

In Bengaluru, K. G. B. Gupta, who has been associated with the Study Group since 1974, facilitates four Study Groups and one Devi Group. T. R. Raghu, who has been involved with Study Groups since 1965, currently attends seven Study Groups. G. N. Seshadri's group has been continuing without a break since 1984. The only breaks are during the yajñas of Guruji and Swami Brahmananda. Krishnan Padiarth and his wife run five Study Groups, each on a different day of the week.

In Mumbai, Narain Bhatia holds five Study Groups in the week, while P. G. Ananthanarayan, at the age of eighty-six, leads one class a week. In Chennai, Hemachandrudu Linga, who has been conducting Study Groups for the past forty years, continues to hold seven classes a week. Many of these senior sevaks are versatile personalities and have been associated with two or all grassroots activities: Bala Vihar, CHYK, and the Study Group. It goes without saying that these senior citizens have grown in knowledge and dedication and are shining role models for the younger generations.

In 1997, Guruji officially recognized the Central Chinmaya Vanaprastha Sansthan (the Senior Citizens organization). Like the other grassroots activity groups, such as Bala Vihar, CHYK, and the Study Group, the Vanaprastha Sansthan has its own set of programs. However, as in the case of the other forums, the main focus remains on the study of the scriptures. In cities where the Vanaprastha Sansthan does not exist, senior citizens continue to be part of the regular adult Study Group.

Looking to 2016 and Beyond

As we approach 2016, the birth centenary of Gurudev, there is a growing recognition that despite the many noble projects undertaken by various centers, the project that was closest to Gurudev's heart was the cultural and spiritual revival of Bharat. For this, he believed, until the very end, that the message of the *Bhagavad-gītā* and the Upaniṣads had to be taken to the farthest corners of this land and beyond. Therefore, strengthening the Study Group for different age groups must remain an important focus of every Mission Center. That is precisely the intention behind Guruji Swami Tejomayananda's concept of Chinmaya Vibhooti, a center for training and inspiring sevaks to make different grassroots-level activities strong and vibrant.

The first international workshop for Study Group Sevaks was held at Chinmaya Vibhooti, Kolwan, from September 8–12, 2009. It served three important purposes:

(1) For the first time, it brought together dedicated Study Group sevaks and sevikās from across India and the globe. Guruji's daily talks on the Study Group enabled those gathered to gain a deeper understanding and appreciation of Gurudev's vast vision and the reason for his emphasizing the importance of the Study Group until the end of his earthly journey. The workshop was both an orientation and a refresher course.

(2) It provided the opportunity for sharing of a wide range of experiences associated with this activity in varying contexts and circumstances. Most importantly, it was the first step in the building of a worldwide network of Study Groups.

(3) It offered a new awareness about the sanctity of this activity and its inherent potential for both individual and group transformation.

Gurudev launched a movement, which has grown into a global organization. The Study Group has played a major role in this process. In this twenty-first century, Guruji's new initiative brings a fresh impetus to this activity in the context of changing times and their associated challenges. Study Group members, old and young, have a sacred responsibility. They have a debt to pay back: to the Ṛṣīs for preserving this knowledge; to Gurudev for presenting it in a language that makes it accessible; and to Chinmaya Mission for nurturing this forum through which we begin our journey into the scriptures. This debt can be paid back only through dedication to the task of sharing this knowledge and by training the next generation to continue the sacred work.

Uttarkashi, 2012. Discussion Group during Guruji's jnana-yajna

Interlaken, Switzerland, 2011. Discussion groups during Guruji's jnana yajna.

PART TWO

The Forest

OPERATE FROM STRENGTH.

THIS STRENGTH COMES FROM:

SINCERE STUDY,

REGULAR ABHYAS,

FIRM CONVICTION,

MISSIONARY ZEAL AND

DEEP DEVOTION

TO WHAT YOU UNDERTAKE TO ACHIEVE.

| SWAMI CHINMAYANANDA |

Multiple Voices: Individual Experiences

XV

The Pioneers

These stories reflect the experiences of some of the many pioneers around the world who took the initiative in their towns and cities to start Study Groups. Each story has its own special flavor, reflecting the personality of the individual and the geographical and cultural contexts of the Study Groups. Yet, there is a common thread through all the stories: that of deep inspiration, devotion, and commitment, both to Gurudev and to the scriptures.

P. G. Ananthanarayan (Uncle Mani) — Mumbai

At the conclusion of his first yajña in Mumbai in 1957, Gurudev took a group of us on a spiritual picnic to Alandi, famous for the samādhi of Sant Jnaneshwar. Early morning sitting under a tree as Śrī Dakṣiṇāmūrti had done, Gurudev said, "Now shoot your questions."

"Swamiji, is there life after death?" came the first question.

Swamiji smiled. "Nobody seems to be concerned about life now!"

After a two-hour question-and-answer session covering a range of practical problems, Gurudev declared that what we needed was a systematic method of studying the scriptures. He suggested that we all begin by reading the *Kena Upaniṣad* as many times as possible. It had already been published with his elaborate commentary.

Six months later, in 1958, in response to a loving personal invitation from Gurudev, a group of us again met him during his transit through Mumbai. He asked how many of us had read *Kena Upaniṣad* at least three times. No hands went up.

"How many of you have read it twice?"

Stillness. No one moved.

"Once?"

One elderly gentleman raised his hand and said, "I read it once, Swamiji."

"Ha! Good. Now tell me how many of you did not read the newspaper for three days at a stretch?"

No hands were raised. We all felt thoroughly ashamed of ourselves.

"So friends," continued Gurudev, "when you do not attach as much importance to the *Kena Upaniṣad* as you do to the newspaper, how do you expect to absorb the knowledge? All right, don't worry. Don't feel ashamed. You are in good company. The mighty Arjuna finds himself in a similar situation in the *Bhagavad-gītā* — of knowing what he should do and yet not being able to do it.[8]

That was our introduction to the necessity of regular study in an organized way. The first study class in Mumbai was formally

---

[8] Arjuna's question: O Kṛṣṇa, impelled by what does man commit sin, even involuntarily, as though driven by force? (*Bhagavad-gītā* II.36)

Śrī Kṛṣṇa's reply: It is desire arising out of the element of rajas, which appears as anger. It is insatiable and grossly wicked. Know this to be the enemy in this case.

instituted in 1963, and Gurudev himself inaugurated it in Śrī B. M. Kamdar's house. A. Parthasarathy (no longer with the Mission) was the moderator. Soon thereafter, Parthasarathy had to undergo an operation and my brother Ramani was asked to take charge of the class. The session was in full swing one evening when we suddenly heard the clipped sounds of wooden slippers fast approaching us. Lo and behold! Gurudev himself appeared in the room!

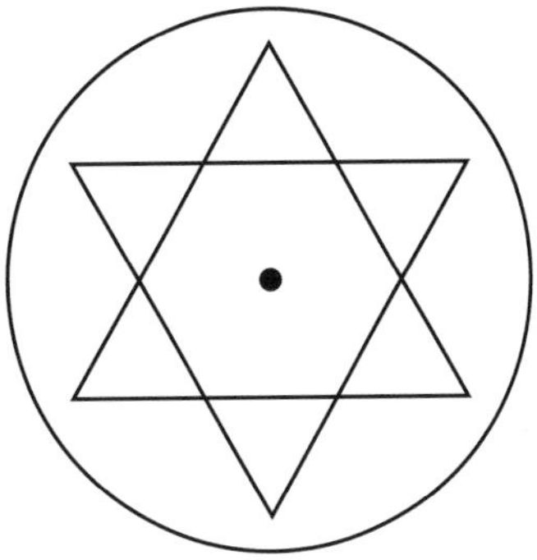

We all shot up to our feet. Gurudev sat down and wanted to know the topic of discussion. It was the mind and intellect. Gurudev's explanation to us is something I will never forget. He drew a triangle. The three sides of the triangle, he said, represent the three instruments through which we function — mind, body, and intellect. The base of the triangle he described as the intellect, the two sides as the body and the mind respectively. We, however, tend to stand on the tip of the pyramid, instead of on the sound base. To illustrate this, he drew a second triangle, this time an inverted one that intersected the first triangle, thus showing us both what we are (the inverted triangle), and what we should be (the first triangle). Then he drew a circle around the two triangles. The circle represents infinity. Together with the center point, it represents the harmonization between *vyaṣṭi* (the individuality) and *samaṣṭi* (the totality). Harmony between the individual BMI and the collective BMI is called mokṣa, freedom from limitation.

That was my initiation to the Study Group by the Guru Himself!

Hemachandrudu Linga, Chennai

I attended Swamiji's yajña in 1962, and soon after joined a Study Group at Mrs. Leela Nambiar's house. Then, because I wanted to get more

1980. ▶
P. G. Ananthanarayana (Uncle Mani) with his Master.

involved, I joined a second Study Group. The latter was the one which had been formed in Chennai immediately after Gurudev's first yajña in 1953 and which led to the formation of Chinmaya Mission. It was still continuing after nine years.

Shortly after I joined the Mission, I was assigned the duty of checking on how the seven or eight Study Groups in the city were running and of getting several new ones started. I gave myself wholeheartedly to this task because, from the moment I first saw Swamiji, I wanted to do something for him. But he did not need anything. What

◀ *Chennai, 1982. Gurudev with Hemachandrudu Linga.*

he had expressed during his very first yajña, and which he repeated each time he came, was that he wanted people to spread the knowledge of Vedānta. So the Study Group became the great motivator in my life.

I would have loved to have gone and studied at Sandeepany Sadhanalaya in Mumbai, but I had financial and other responsibilities, and these continued until I was about fifty-two. So I devoted myself to the study of Sanskrit and to this great knowledge, and gradually came to have a reasonably good grasp of both. I must also mention that I did not strictly follow the prescribed system of study because I realized that most people could not sustain that scheme. It is really meant for those who are deeply motivated, because to remain engaged in such deep study over an extended period of time requires great commitment.

In 1985, I ventured to conduct Study Groups with the Yuva Kendra. At one time I was holding five Yuva Kendra classes with a total of about 125 youth. One of these classes lasted for seven years. Many swamis and brahmacārīs have been part of these Yuva Kendra classes.

Currently, I conduct seven Study Groups. Involvement in this activity has transformed my life. You see, when you take classes every day, you have to prepare for them. Therefore, from morning to evening wherever you are, whatever you are doing, you are thinking about the topic. During the class, many questions are asked. They remain in your mind and you keep reflecting on them. So these topics become the whole day's meditation.

Since I am in the construction business. Gurudev used me as an instrument in the construction of the Śrī Rāma Temple at Sidhbari and the Chinmaya Vidyalaya at New Delhi. I always felt that the construction business was my hobby and that the Study Group was my life.

***Ācārya Uma Jeyarasasingam**, Los Altos, California*

I first heard Gurudev in Malaysia in 1965 but personally met him in 1967 during his yajña in that country. On that occasion, he gave me a carton full of his books and told me to read them and to write to him if I didn't understand. I brought the box home but did not get to read the books, because shortly thereafter, I got married and moved with my husband to San Francisco. The books moved with me.

Discovering a Study Group in San Francisco, my husband and I joined it and were the only Indians in the group. When Beth Patterson, the American group leader, withdrew from this activity for personal reasons, the Study Group came to an end. It was then that I started reading the books that Gurudev had given me. I also began writing to him. He advised me to take the Postal Lesson Course, which I completed in 1969.

From 1971, Gurudev visited the Greater Bay Area every year,

▲

San Francisco, 1969. L to R. Uma Jeyarasasingam with daughter Gayathri, Maya Menon, Beverly Simmons, K. Jeyarasasingam. Kneeling in front of cake is Solange Berg whose husband Bob Berg (not in picture) was a founding member of CMW Board of Directors.

holding spiritual family camps and yajñas. It was at the conclusion of his yajña in 1973 that he encouraged me to form a Study Group in San Francisco. I was full of trepidation because I felt I did not know enough. Gurudev reassured me saying, "You are not teaching anything. You are just convening the class and moderating it. I know you don't know anything!" "Moreover," he added, "you are going to learn along with them. All you do, if they can't understand and if you cannot explain, is to write it down. When I come next time I'll answer the questions." So, we all kept a record of our study in our notebooks.

I started with a small group of seven people who would meet in my home. All of them were Americans who had attended Gurudev's yajña. There were Jews, Christians, and agnostics. Gurudev's instructions on the format of the class were very clear, "Don't introduce chanting of prayers to the students. They are all Americans. They should not misunderstand and think that you are trying to convert them. That is not our purpose. You chant the invocation and start the discussion right away." The group ran for eight years and we met *thrice* a week.

Five years later, in 1978, my family moved to a home in Los Altos, about forty miles south of San Francisco. There we formed a new Study Group with devotees who had attended Gurudev's talks at Stanford University. We adopted the scheme of study set up by Gurudev and continued for the next ten years until 1988.

Pūjya Gurudev would hold satsaṅga with all the Study Group members every year. On one such occasion, as the Study Group leader, I read out to him a question from a member of my group: "In *Vivekacūḍāmaṇi*, while discussing the work of Ādi Śaṅkara, we all assume that he is a realized person. How do we know that he is actually realized? I can't accept that."

Gurudev looked at me and said: "This is not your doubt. Let the one who has the doubt ask the question." So the person who had raised the question read it out again. Looking at him with kindness and love Gurudev responded, "You are right. You do not know whether Ādi Śaṅkara is realized, and hence your question. It is a very legitimate doubt. Ādi Śaṅkara was an established thinker and a man of knowledge of that time. He explained as best as he could to those who were present before him. Today we are studying the same text as generations of students before us have done. Can you offer a better explanation than the one he has given us?"

"No sir," came the reply.

"All right. Shall we then listen to his explanations for now, and if you come up with an alternate explanation which is acceptable to all scholars, then it can be replaced. Is that acceptable to you?"

"Yes, Swamiji."

In 1989, Swami Tejomayananda was posted as the Ācārya of Chinmaya Mission, San Jose. On Gurudev's advice, I suspended the Study Group to attend Guruji's classes. So, until Guruji's departure for India after the *mahāsamādhi* of Gurudev, all of us in the Study Group attended Guruji's classes regularly. These were held every day, beginning at 6:30 A.M. A second class would take place at 10:00 A.M., and a third in the evening. In that way, I did the entire Vedānta course with Guruji. In between the classes, I attended to other Mission work at the San Jose Center. In 1993, after Guruji's departure, I resumed with the Study Group in my home and also started a second one at Milipitas, fifteen miles away. These two Study Groups continue even today.

I remember asking Gurudev in 1985 whether we were ready to have an āśrama in our area. He replied, "Four walls do not make an āśrama. You evolve spiritually along with the others, and the āśrama will form around you. That is the significance of an āśrama." It was clear. We had to create dedicated spiritual workers, and, for that, he advised us to continue with the Study Group. "And," he added, "the workers should be inspired by the scriptures and not by me. And this inspiration must lead to their transformation. No person can make them transform."

***Aviva Keller**, Zurich, Switzerland*

After I completed the Vedānta Course in Mumbai in 1983, Gurudev encouraged me to go back to Switzerland, complete my university education, and then work in the world and assimilate this knowledge. He also recommended that I take a Study Group so that I would not forget what I had learned at the āśrama.

When I finally settled down in Switzerland, I joined the Study Group that had been organized by Krishnan Padiarth (now in

Bengaluru) and took over the group when Padiarth returned to India in 1989. I continue to lead that group even today.

The class is held in English, which is not our mother tongue. However, since the books are in English, I have to ensure that people read them. I don't want to add my own interpretations inadvertently. I have always wanted the group members to get the ideas of Gurudev directly from the text. The fact that we hold the class in English also necessitates some changes in the recommended structure of the class. There are many who are very shy to read out aloud in English or who simply find it too demanding to read through pages of commentaries in a foreign language as homework. So, for example, if we are doing a chapter of the *Gītā*, we chant the verse, then we read the translation, and then I give a summary of Gurudev's commentary. After I have summarized the main thrust of that verse, a volunteer reads one or two paragraphs of the commentary, which I feel are of great importance. Then, if someone wishes to add something, he or she does so. At this point, some people have questions and doubts and we have a discussion. On the whole, members of the Friday Study Group are advanced and dedicated seekers and very genuinely support one another.

◀ *Zurich, 2013. Front row L to R – Andrea Huttenegger (pink top), Katherine Kaposzy, Aviva Keller (yellow top), Marie Therese Stoler, and Katherine Jegger. Back row L to R – Niranjan Pal Singh and Mr. and Mrs. Green.*

Zurich, 2013. The Study Group of Yoga teachers, L to R – Tarini Anita Frei, dog Jai, Aviva Keller, Ursula Wettstein, Marian Mittelholzer, Katherine Kaposzy. Jai the dog is a regular and peaceful member of the group.

For the last few years, I have also been conducting a second Study Group. This is a group of yoga teachers aged between twenty and forty years. They are very motivated to learn Sanskrit and study the *Bhagavad-gītā*. We meet just once a month; it is a German-speaking group. When we started, we had the problem of finding a German translation of the *Gītā*. So we settled for a translation by a German professor. I supplement that with the ideas and insights of Gurudev's commentary. Hopefully, Gurudev's *Gītā* will become available in German some day.

Since the last twenty-two years that I have been conducting the first class, we have completed the whole syllabus — the old syllabus.[9] Gurudev told me to just keep on doing this, even if people came and went, and even if they felt that it was just entertainment. What I had

[9] Guruji Swami Tejomayananda has included some additional texts in the syllabus laid down by Gurudev. These include *Upadeśa-sāra* and *Saddarśanam* by Bhagavan Ramana Marashi and four short texts by Guruji himself. See Appendix.

to remember, he said, was that it was my sādhanā. And this sādhanā, I must say, has been most helpful for me because I am working and living in this very fast-paced material world. The Friday class compels me to devote one full day of the week to my spiritual pursuit. Without that, I don't know how I would have managed any regular sādhanā at all.

On Fridays, which is the day the Study Group takes place, I spend the entire day meditating and fasting. I try not to eat on that day and restrict myself to just some tea. It's nice to be able to forget about these things for at least one day of the week, because, when you have received a gift like the Sandeepany course, you have to ensure that you safeguard it. In the environment in which we live, it is so easy to lose it by just being scattered. So, Friday has become a day of safekeeping; it is my day for turning inward and being in contact with these great teachings.

In August 2011, Guruji came to Interlaken, Switzerland, for the first camp organized by the German-speaking Swiss group. Many people from both my Study Groups participated, and the younger lot was quite involved. It is not possible to gauge the subtle impact of this experience in the lives and thoughts of the participants who came for the first time; even one young woman is interested in joining the Vedānta course in Mumbai. The others have found the orientation, clarity, the spiritual atmosphere of the Study Group, and the yajña experience very inspiring and helpful in their own lives.

Paula Spronk, *Vught, Holland*

I was introduced to Vedānta and the work of Swami Chinmayananda by Daniela Schwarz in Zurich. Her radiance and inner peace drew me to her. The two of us began to meet several times a week to read some of Gurudev's writings and commentaries on the scriptures. In 1984, I met Gurudev for the first time when I accompanied Daniela to a camp in Sidhbari.

On my return to Zurich, I joined the Study Group that Aviva

Keller conducted, and I also continued my regular study meetings with Daniela Schwarz. Two years later, in 1986, I joined the 6th Vedānta Course at Sandeepany Sadhanalaya with Guruji Swami Tejomayananda as Ācārya. Before that, however, I got engaged to Frank Spronk, also a devotee of Gurudev. Swami Chinmayananda's advice to me was, "First you study, then you marry."

Adjusting to my new life in Mumbai was challenging. In May 1987, Gurudev lovingly wrote, "Without any mental dissipation, with all devotion, you study sincerely; the knowledge of Vedānta can change your entire personality and, so, your destiny. Apply yourself for two and a half years steadily, devotedly."

On the completion of the course, I received another letter from Gurudev, with this advice: "Try to hold classes wherever you are, every evening, based upon one text or the other. Don't worry about the number of people listening. Keep the Lord's picture in front of you and talk to Him."

I returned to Europe in 1989, and Frank and I were married the same year. Shortly thereafter, I started a Study Group on *Ātma Bodha* in English. About twelve people in the age group of twenty-five to seventy years started meeting at our home. They came from different professional backgrounds — a music school director, a nurse, a musician, and others — but all of them were deeply interested, and the commentary of Gurudev fascinated them. However, the experience was very different from what I had seen in India. Here, neither had anyone met Gurudev nor had they even heard of him before this study. Advaita Vedānta was something quite unknown, and the general attitude toward religion and spiritual groups was one of skepticism.

The Western mind also has certain preconceived notions about the Self, which are hard to change. And the topic of our study was *Ātma Bodha*, the knowledge of the Self. After concluding the text, one participant seemed to be very happy and clear about all that had

▲

Vught, Holland, July 2012. Guruji with the Spronk Family. Frank Spronk (extreme left), behind him are Paula, son Anton Mecht, and Frank's mother. On the right side are older son Gerard Hans and Frank's father.

been discussed. I realized that he took the purely physically bound psychological Self as the Ātman. This impression was for me a warning about the necessity to be very specific when one talks about Ātman if one is to avoid any misunderstanding. The Self is pure Consciousness, objectless Awareness, and does not "sit" inside the body. The Western mind very often seems to have a very different notion about the Self.

Despite such challenges, I derived strength from Gurudev. He guided me in spirit, because I, as a little person, would never have had the stamina to carry the group through to the completion of the text. Westerners are very concerned about their individuality. A certain pride of learning and education makes people very sure of themselves and a little rigid in their ideas. I was conscious of the ever-present danger of getting entangled in mere intellectual discourse and discussion. Fortunately, I was blessed with the inspiration of Gurudev, and that was my anchor. Knowledge had to come from Him through me, the Study Group moderator. Therefore, the tuning with the Guru was of utmost importance. Until today, my prayer is that he will talk through me.

Soon after, we moved to Vught, a town south of Amsterdam, where our two sons, Gerard Hans and Anton Mecht were born. Our home became the regular study setting for all four of us. When the children started to understand English, I started reading and discussing Vedāntic articles and texts like *Ātma Bodha* and *Kindle Life* with them. Before Gerard, the older son, moved to Amsterdam for his music studies at the conservatory, we had a few years when we studied together almost every evening. We listened to talks by Gurudev on the *Gītā*, and by Guruji on different texts, and on weekends we would study these texts. Together, we have studied *Manaḥ-śodhanam*, *Jñānasāraḥ*, *Upadeśa-sāra*, *Amṛtabindu Upaniṣad*, *Kaṭha Upaniṣad*, *Yoga Vasiṣṭha*, the *Bhagavad-gītā*, *Vivekacūḍāmaṇi*, and others. We would read the text and reflect upon it together in the English language.

In preparation for Guruji's first yajña in Holland in July 2012, we started holding an open discussion group every alternate Saturday. For each occasion, we chose a specific theme, such as 'the Spiritual Quest,' 'the Qualifications of a Seeker,' 'The Vision of Advaita,' and so on. Alongside, we continued with our weekly Study Group of *Manaḥ-śodhanam* and that of the *Yoga Vasiṣṭha* every alternate week. Several ladies have been regular attendees of these Study Groups for the last few years. The books of Gurudev and Guruji have been the focus of our study. Through my sharing, I try to build a bridge between the East and West, between the Indian and Christian religious traditions. Vedānta being a universal spiritual wealth, we would like to share it with all.

Currently, we have two Study Groups on Saturdays (doing *Self-Unfoldment* and *Vivekacūḍāmaṇi*) and several one-on-one meetings throughout the week based on different texts.

Gurudev united four jīvas temporarily in a family unit to grow together in sādhanā and spread the Divine Song. It looks like this Spronk Family is growing into a Chinmaya unit in Holland. Our house is a place for music and study. It is His. We are His. Our children are His.

EXTRACT FROM A LETTER BY GURUDEV TO PAULA SPRONK

APRIL 1990

Continue sharing your knowledge of the Vedānta Truth with others all through your life. Never miss even a single day of reading a bit of the *Gītā* and/or Upaniṣad. Try meditation daily.

EXTRACT FROM A LETTER BY GURUJI TO PAULA SPRONK.

SEPTEMBER 1990, SANDEEPANY SAN JOSE, CALIFORNIA

Bees come where flowers are blossomed with their sweet fragrance. Seekers of knowledge will come to you likewise.

Paris 1993. Gurudev with Paula Spronk and Gerard Hans. The last meeting.

XVI

Some Inspiring Study Group Members

Below are a few of the many stories that members of different Study Groups have shared with us. While some have been role models, others offer interesting insights into the power of the Study Group to bring about transformation. Four of these individuals were associated with Gurudev; another connected with him only through his commentaries. He drew them all to him, and each was deeply touched and transformed by the contact.

The late Harkishan Lal Soni, *Bengaluru (As told by G. N. Seshadri, his Study Group Leader)*

Harkishan Lal Soni joined the Study Group at our home on August 2, 1993. A seventy-one-year-old widower, he had been a Colonel in the Army and, after retirement, had run his own business in Pune and New Delhi. Until his move to Bengaluru in 1986, he had had no association with Chinmaya Mission or Vedānta philosophy.

Soniji's story is one of extraordinary self-transformation in the evening of life. From the very first day in the Study Group, his attention, devotion, and dedication to scriptural study were extraordinary. In the ten years that he was a part of this group, Soniji's vairāgya (dispassion) grew visibly deeper, leading him to withdraw gradually from the world. Giving away his television set to a local school, he even stopped reading newspapers and spent his time in scriptural study and meditation. The radiance and purity of his inner personality were reflected in his outer environment. His home was immaculately clean and orderly.

So total was Soniji's identification with Chinmaya Mission, with Gurudev, and with Swami Brahmanandaji that he began to celebrate August 2, the day he had joined the Study Group, as his birthday. To use his own words, "Since I entered the Study Group, I am reborn."

The ultimate test of his knowledge came when he was diagnosed with lung cancer. That he had completely assimilated Upaniṣadic wisdom through study and reflection was made manifest in his ability to detach from any identification with the body. Through his illness, he repeatedly assured us that he did not suffer. Even during bouts in the hospital, his regularity in spiritual study remained undisturbed. When he was discharged, his routine of study, meditation, evening walks, and attendance at the Study Group would resume as before.

On Monday, February 10, 2003, barely five days before he left his body, Soniji attended the Study Group. He spoke to the group on the *Kaṭha Upaniṣad*, the text under study, which is a dialogue between a young seeker and the Lord of Death. His complete serenity in the face of impending death, his joy at being with the Study Group and discussing a subject in which he reveled, was a living testimony to us of the power of Vedānta. He was a true jñāna yogī.

On February 14, 2003, Soniji felt physically very weak. We knew that his journey in the body was coming to an end. When my wife and I suggested that we stay with him for the night, he politely and firmly refused saying that the Lord would take care of him. His devotion and surrender were those of a true bhakti yogī.

The next day, on the instructions of Pūjya Swami Brahmanandaji, we drove him to the Chinmaya Mission Hospital. In front of the Deena

Bandhu Temple, he asked for some tender coconut water. Taking a few sips, he said, "Hari Om," and breathed his last. His last rites were performed under the guidance of, and in the holy presence of, Pūjya Swami Brahmanandaji.

In his memory, every year, Chinmaya Mission Bangalore organizes a special Sadhana Day for Study Group Members. Generally it is held in February to coincide with Soniji's death anniversary. On that day, the thirty Study Groups in Bangalore gather together, having studied a specific text prescribed by Swami Brahmanandaji over the previous two months. New discussion groups are formed by drawing members from diverse Study Groups, and each new group is given a portion of the text to reflect upon and discuss. In the afternoon, one member from each group does a presentation of the group's experience and understanding. Swami Brahmananda wraps up the program with his own comments. The program lasts for about four-to-five hours and includes lunch.

Drs. T. S. Chidambaram and Kamala Chidambaram, Chennai

T. S. Chidambaram: Our association with Chinmaya Mission began in 1982 when we attended a jñāna yajña by Professor Vasudevan in Chennai. He was a senior member of the Mission, besides being a Professor of English and Head of the Department at Vaishnava College. We were both so inspired by his talks that we decided to take up the serious study of the scriptures. However, we had very little spare time. I am a pediatrician and my wife is a gynecologist.

When I asked Professor Vasudevan if both of us could come to his house and study with him, he decided to conduct a Study Group for us in our home. The only time available to us was 5:30 in the morning, for we had long hours of work. So, for the next thirteen years, Professor Vasudevan led our Study Group diligently and devotedly. He would cycle all the way to our home, and at 5:30 A.M. sharp, he would begin chanting Om. Classes were held twice a week. We plunged straight into the *Bhagavad-gītā* on Saturdays and into *Vivekacūḍāmaṇi* on Tuesdays. We were a group of about eight people.

Over the years, we completed the *Bhagavad-gītā, Vivekacūḍāmaṇi,* all the Upaniṣads, *Nārada Bhakti Sūtra,* and a few other texts. We did not strictly follow the syllabus of the Mission. Whatever Professor Vasudevan wanted, he taught us. Then, in the late 1990s, a few years after Gurudev's mahāsamādhi, Professor Vasudevan informed us that we did not need to attend Study Groups anymore. It was only then that we started holding our own classes.

Sidhbari, 1991. Gurudev with Drs. T.S. Chidambaram and Kamala Chidambaram.

Kamala Chidambaram: After we became involved in scriptural study, we began to invite Gurudev to our home for bhikṣā every time he visited Chennai. In 1990, we went to Sidhbari for a camp where we were shown a documentary film on Dr. Kshama Metre's work. Gurudev asked me what I thought of it. I replied that I wished something like that could happen at Tamaraipakkam.[10] Gurudev looked at me and thundered, "How can such a thing happen when there are selfish doctors like you who only want to earn money?"

Now, I had heard that such a scolding from Gurudev normally precedes a great blessing! So I just stood there, unaffected by the tone of his voice and his words. I was waiting for that blessing. Nothing came that day. He simply dismissed me. Everyone around me was watching me carefully, expecting me to burst into tears. But I knew something good would follow.

The next day, we were offering bhikṣā to Gurudev. As we were leading him to the dining hall, he put his hand on my shoulder and said, "You know, Tamaraipakkam is your *karma bhūmi* (place for you to offer selfless service). So, you do your karma yoga there. Don't expect anything from those patients. You are there only to serve them. So work hard. They will not listen to your advice. But it is not for treating them that you will go there. So, go and take care of Tamaraipakkam."

From that day onward, for the next twenty-two years, I offered sevā there every Sunday. Since 2011, there has been an in-house doctor stationed at CORD Tamaraipakkam.

Krishnan and Ammini Padiyath, Bengaluru

Krishnan Padiyath: I met Gurudev in Zurich in 1973. Shortly after meeting Annemarie, my German wife, Gurudev named her Ammini, a typical name from Kerala. In 1974, we became involved in assisting Adolf Hodel to organize Gurudev's annual talks in Zurich, and, in 1978, we took over this responsibility and continued for nearly ten years.

---

[10] Tamaraipakkam, a village situated forty kilometers from Chennai, is the location of an imposing Śiva Liṅga temple, an old-age home, a charitable medical center, a free village school, playgrounds, and cowsheds, spread over eight acres of land, all established by Chinmaya Mission.

I started a Study Group in 1977–78 at the home of the late Elizabeth Hallauer who would host Gurudev in Switzerland. We were only four or five people in the group. In the mid-1980s, Aviva Keller returned from Sandeepany Mumbai, and Gurudev asked me to hand over the moderator's role to her. I continued to attend the class that she now led until I returned to India in 1989.

Wittingen, Switzerland, 1973. Gurudev with Krishnan and Ammini Padiyath.

Ammini Padiyath: Krishnan would talk to everybody about the Study Group: in the office, in public places, and even on the train. Most of the people laughed at him but a few got very interested. He would invite people to Gurudev's talks and several did come.

Krishnan also went once a month to Geneva (four hours away by fast train, hence an eight-hour round trip) for a one-hour Study Group there. He did that for a couple of years.

Krishnan: Gurudev asked us, "Why do you rot in this cold climate here? Come and do some Mission work in India." Since I was good at conducting Study Groups, he suggested that I continue serving by doing just that. So we returned to India in 1989. I was fifty-two years old.

Ammini: India was quite a change for me from this beautiful, small, well-organized Switzerland. But the move was a very good decision. It was a decision that came from inside. I was a librarian by profession and I had to read a lot. But I had reached a point where I was only interested in reading spiritual literature and reflecting on it. So I would not have been able to do justice to my profession. India was a little challenging because it enabled us to gauge how much we had really learned, how much detachment we really had toward material things.

It is in India that I got actively involved in the Study Group. However, years of mananam (reflection) had preceded this. Ever since I met Swami Chinmayananda, I was reading and reflecting upon his writings. I had also completed the postal Vedānta course. We lived a very disciplined life in Switzerland, getting up everyday at 4:30 A.M. to meditate, because Swamiji constantly emphasized the importance of meditation — śravaṇam, mananam, and nididhyāsanam.

Krishnan: Presently, we are both sevaks of six Study Groups which all meet once a week. The Study Group gives meaning and joy to life. It ensures that there is never any monotony. We are constantly striving, not for fame, wealth, or recognition, but simply for the satisfaction of doing what we are doing. My wife is also a source of great motivation.

Ammini: Every morning after meditation, we sit together and do our svādhyāya. Today, it was *Kindle Life*. Even though we know the text very well, we still read it again because there is always some new insight to be gained. I read and Krishnan listens because he has a chronic throat ailment. If something is not clear, we discuss it. There are so many things that we have heard together, read together, and reflected upon together.

XVII

Influence of Study Group on Professional Life

This chapter is a testimony to the practicality and applicability of Vedānta in everyday life. The many voices that speak in these pages represent a wide range of professions. For each one, the individual and collective study of the scriptures has lead to greater clarity of purpose, conviction, and commitment, resulting in a more meaningful and fulfilling professional life. In some cases, the workplace became a source for recruiting Study Group members.

G. N. Seshadri, *Director, Shandilya Institute of Nurturing Excellence, Bengaluru*

I was working as an engineer, when, in 1979, I underwent training in Attitudinal Development and Leadership by a trainer from the Dale Carnegie Institute of the U.S.A. The trainer, who was from India, had attended many of Gurudev's talks, and he introduced me to the work of Gurudev. That's when I joined Chinmaya Mission and enrolled for Vigyan Mandir classes. In 1981, the deep understanding of our scriptures inspired me to develop management-training programs on soft skills and behavioral sciences based on this knowledge. My wife and I also started a Study Group in our house in 1984, which continues to meet to this day.

2013. Bengaluru. G. N. Sesahdri's Study Group. From L to R – Lalitha Seshadri, Jayashri Kireeti, Srikanta Prasad, G. N. Seshadri, T. R. Raghu.

The success of the training programs I developed eventually lead me to found the Shandilya Institute of Nurturing Excellence (SHINE) in 1996. SHINE has trained over four hundred thousand professionals of various levels through more than four thousand training programs at the time of this writing.

I insist that all our faculty members study *Kindle Life* thoroughly before venturing into actual training. The Mission Pledge is also part of our training program. We have taken permission from the Mission to do so, and we acknowledge the Mission, but only at the end of the program. That is because we have participants from various faiths, and it is only once they have understood the deep significance of the words of the Pledge that we tell them where it is from. In fact, if we live by the Chinmaya Mission Pledge in daily life, we don't require any management training.

Several people whom I have met and worked with professionally have eventually become members of the Study Group. One of them is a young woman called Lalitha Sairam. Seeing her exceptional abilities when I first met her in the context of one of our programs, I suggested a training career to her. She joined me as my assistant and became a competent trainer in her own right with our organization.

What impressed her most was our Chinmaya Mission approach, and she happily joined our Study Group. Shortly thereafter, she and her husband, a top IT professional with DELL, started a Study Group in their home.

About five years later, Lalitha became pregnant with her third child. Throughout her pregnancy, she remained deeply involved in spiritually related professional and personal activities. The day the child was born, her husband Sairam called us and announced: "Chinmaya is born." The baby had been named after Gurudev. Today, they are in the U.S. and Chinmaya is about seven years old.

Jayashri Kireeti, Architect, Bengaluru

I had been in the Study Group for two years, when a single word, *tanmayāḥ*, in the *Nārada Bhakti Sūtra* (v. 70), set me thinking. Tanmayāḥ, in brief, signifies reveling in the Self constantly, as a man of wisdom (jñānī) does. This inspired me to conceptualize a design for my house, which depicted, in symbolic fashion, the journey of a seeker (sādhaka) as well as the supreme goal that he or she strives for.

Facing the house from the road, you see an undulating rock and mud compound wall with a large green gate. The undulating wall signifies the ups and downs of daily life. The huge green gate looks intimidating. Its scale indicates the beauty and grandeur of the life ahead (as a sādhaka). The hesitation to enter is symbolic of the self-doubt most people experience before taking the plunge into Vedānta.

On entering, one finds oneself at the lowest level of the property, symbolic of animal man (see *Kindle Life*). Two stone steps, followed by a curved stone pathway with a pergola overhead, and a wooden bench en route, lead to the entrance door. The stone steps and pathway indicate the initial efforts of a sādhaka on the journey, while the bench signifies the periods of rest along the way. The overhead pergola suggests the constant grace of the Lord upon the seeker during these initial efforts.

A canopy covering the entrance door signifies how dharma protects him who abides by it (dharmo rakṣati rakṣitaḥ). The door, representing the entrance into a divine way of life, opens onto a large sunbathed green rain court. The source of sunlight, a large skylight, remains hidden at this point. To the left, there is a semi-dark sitting place for visitors. In the center stands a circular staircase. The invisible center of the staircase represents the Self. It is the point from which the whole design emerges, even as the whole manifested world emerges from the Self without being perceived by the BMI. The semi-dark sitting area on the left is a place close to the center, or Self, and is the space for higher contemplations. This is where we have our weekly Study Group meeting.

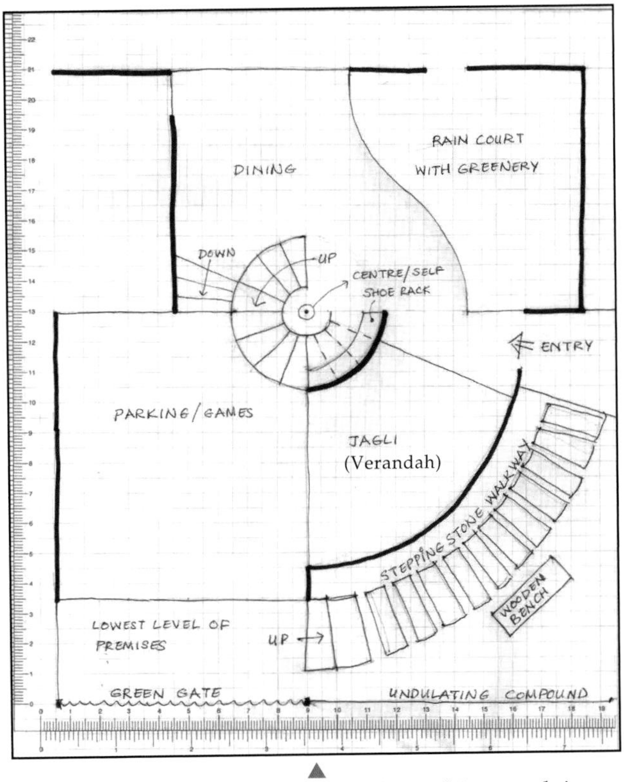

The design of Jayashri Kireeti's house 'Tanmayāḥ in Bengaluru.

At the foot of the circular staircase is the shoe rack. Removing one's shoes to climb the wide comfortable steps, well lit by the overhead skylight, is symbolic of surrender of the ego. Thereafter, with the surrender of the ego, the consequent ease in sādhanā and clarity of purpose elevate the sādhaka. The steps wind around the center and, on reaching the upstairs level, one glimpses the source of light that sunbathes the rain court. This point represents the end of the sādhaka's journey.

The design enables us, the residents, and also a few sensitive guests, to perceive divinity and be constantly reminded of the ultimate goal of life and the path that leads to it. We have named the house Tanmaya.

Rudite Emir, *President, Orca Corporation, Mountain View, California*

The Study Group gave me a means for keeping the Divine uppermost in my mind throughout my daily activities. With the Study Group as my weekly reminder of what is most important in my life, I used all of life's activities, including my professional life, as a 'laboratory' for putting into practice the principles that Vedānta had revealed to me. During many of those early years, I was employed at several Silicon Valley companies that were just getting off the ground. That meant that we were working long hours and under a lot of stress. The challenge was how to keep my balance — an inner equipoise — through all of the many pressures that came my way. I always tried to keep the Vedāntic teaching in mind, to use it to stabilize my mind during the hectic workday, much like a ship's ballast that prevents it from keeling over. Vedānta helped me immensely.

One Study Group that I led for a good many years consisted of people I had met in my professional life and who had become inspired by Vedānta. This group came about without my planning it. It was in the 1980s when I was the head of a department in a Silicon Valley computer company. One day, a young man who worked in my department, standing in the doorway of my office, said something like this, "There's something about the way you do your work, the way you approach people, that is different from the usual. I am trying to figure out what it is." I said to myself, "If he has put his foot in the (metaphorical) doorway, gingerly trying to open the door, I will certainly help him open it wide!" And, so I did — by starting to talk to him about Vedānta. He was keenly interested, and soon thereafter, I formed a new Study Group, which included him and several other computer professionals who had shown interest. The one who had opened the door for discussion, a man named Ben Passarelli, was a devoted member of my Study Group for many years and has attended almost all the Dharma Sevak courses offered in California.

A few years later, another Chinmaya Mission member, Srinivas Sukumar (Chinmaya Mission San Diego), and I decided to start a professional group that promoted functioning with integrity and wisdom in the corporate world, bringing a spiritual dimension into the workplace. Gradually, other people who had similar leanings were brought into the group, which we named CompassioNet. At first, we thought that we would create some kind of an entity that would offer workshops, consultancies, and so on, but that never happened. What happened instead is that individual people in the growing group contacted each other for collaborating on projects, because we all had the same orientation and loved working together. Some members initiated innovative social activism projects, both in India and in the U.S. Several members have published books, among them *From Smart to Wise: Acting and Leading with Wisdom* (2013) by Prasad Kaipa, a regular member of our group, and Navi Radjou. These accomplishments aside, we realized that we basically enjoyed getting tougher *simply to be together*, that is, to be in satsaṅga with one another. When we meet, we talk about our work lives, but always in the context of the spiritual life. And we continue to learn from each other — and even from ourselves, simply by having given voice to a quiet urge within.

Recently we have introduced the next generation of students of Vedānta to the group and are amazed at the richness they bring to our conversation. There are young people who have attended Bala Vihar and Yuva Kendra during their formative years and are now applying everything they have heard and experienced in the Mission to their daily lives. Technologically savvy, they want to change the world in ways and through means that the older generation cannot even imagine. When we listen to them, we are awestruck at the depth of their understanding and desire to make this world a better place.

Professor K. Sreeharsha, *Formerly of San Jose State University, California*

I see commonality in my professional field and in my study of Vedānta. Vedānta asks me to look within. Likewise, my professional life — material science and engineering — is also about looking at the inside of materials. Vedānta talks of name, form, activity, and the possibility of change (nāma, rūpa, guṇa, sambandha, and so on). That is also what I see in materials: name, form, and potential for activity, properties and ability to change. So, the concepts are exactly the same, with different terminologies.

When you look at a person, he or she is not just what you see. It is the same with materials. When you look at a material, it is not what it appears to be. Then you want to change it, like you want to change yourself. Just as you want to make yourself into something better, so do you seek to do the same with materials. I can consider myself as a material. In a nutshell, there is a universal type of analysis that is common to both science and spirituality.

Daniela Badea, *Finance and Accounting Manager, Yazaki Romania Ploiesti, Romania*

Having completed the Dharma Sevak Course in 2011 at Coimbatore, I have started Study Groups in my country to spread the knowledge of Vedānta. In my company, I am preparing a booklet of short Vedāntic tales as an educational tool for workers (we have 4,600 people working for us). It includes several stories from the Purāṇas. These offer advice on the art of living, right thinking, the importance of family values, God, religion, science, and so on.

I have also started a big project of translating Ādi Śaṅkara's works and other Vedāntic texts into Romanian. So far, *Tattva Bodhaḥ, Ātma Bodhaḥ, Bhaja Govindam, Vākya Vṛtti* and *Dṛg-dṛśya Viveka* have been completed. I am working with a team of translators, and we are in discussions with a spiritual publishing house to get these books published. Simultaneously, I am trying to get sponsorship for this project from some big Romanian companies (like the one I am working in). Another project on the way is to create an opera on Gurudev. This is my dream and my contribution to my country.

Douglas Boodt, *Attorney at Law, Illinois (Study Group sevak at Chicago)*

I've realized at work that you don't have to get angry and that you don't have to be belligerent when you are representing a client. So many of my colleagues are not fun people to deal with. As you know, attorneys have a certain reputation, especially American attorneys. I have realized, as Swamiji [Gurudev] says, that you must do the best for your client and leave the rest. I have understood that everything is not in my control. There are other factors that are also involved. This has brought a certain peace to what I do, and it has reduced the stress levels in my professional life.

Dr. Aviva Keller, *Psychologist, Zurich, Switzerland*

This knowledge and sādhanā has had a profound impact on my attitude at work. People come to me when they have conflicts, or when they are searching for their path, or when they are in difficult relationships. As a psychologist, I regard every person who comes to my clinic as a manifestation of the Self. I don't look at people as psychopathological cases on two legs, but as divine manifestations who come to share a problem. This attitude, I find, communicates itself to the other person, and I feel that we begin from a more comfortable and humane base. When you go into the witnessing mode, then, even if you are not a perfect person yourself, that attitude helps other people.

***Darren Pereira**, Success Coach, SUCCESS INTEGRATED, Melbourne, Australia*

My professional life and my growth in Chinmaya Mission developed simultaneously. As my involvement in the CHYK Study Group grew, my dissatisfaction deepened with my job as an accountant at KPMG. After much personal angst and disapproval from my parents, I decided to make the big move and quit KPMG to follow my svabhāva. I wanted to become an international speaker, a bold call for a depressed accountant! That was in 1997.

I went back to university to complete a Graduate Diploma in Vocational Education and Training. During my mid-semester break, I attended an International Family Camp with Guruji at Sidhbari. This experience was a huge turning point in my life. Subsequently, taking CHYK classes and attending all of Swami Swaroopananda's yajñas, workshops and camps became a major priority for me.

Upon completing my diploma, I joined a company called Leadership Management Australia, which was a behavior-change training organization. Within four months, I managed to be the worst performer in Australia! Once again, I had failed. But the knowledge I was gaining from the Study Group kept me strong and I was determined not to give up! So I approached another franchise and was once again employed on the same conditions. Seven months later, I had become the number one Business Development Manager and Leadership Coach in Australia! I quickly gained local and international recognition.

One day, when talking to Swami Swaroopananda, I dropped a five-cent coin. Swamiji bent down and picked it up. He put the coin in my hand, and covering my hand with his, said, "Darren turn these five cents into five million." That was huge for me. If my Guru thought I could achieve success, then I knew it was going to happen.

Not long after, I ended up making one of the biggest decisions of my life and started my own business at age 27. I called it SUCCESS INTEGRATED (which is based on the concept of integrating the mind and intellect). At that point I was heavily involved with the CHYKs, most of whom were just out of high school. To make the CHYK class more interesting and engaging, I ran mini-workshops. The CHYKs really enjoyed them and suggested that I run these sessions at their former high schools, because this was a message that students needed to hear. Some of these CHYKs had been captains or prefects in their schools. They personally introduced and endorsed me to the teachers, who subsequently invited me to speak to their students. I could never have guessed that this would lead me to where I am nine years later, running approximately 150 seminars a year, most of these booked twelve months in advance. I now speak to about 20,000 students, parents, and teachers a year.

My signature program is titled SHAPE YOUR DESTINY, and it is specifically designed to help people gain a direction and purpose in their lives, that is, to discover their svabhāva. I attribute most of my personal breakthroughs and success to Gurudev and Swami Swaroopananda. The courage to live my passion crystalized over time, and would not have been possible without the inspiration I received from regularly attending and applying what I learned from the Chinmaya Mission Study Group.

Dr. Kamala Chidambaram, Obstetrician and Gynecologist, Chennai

As an obstetrician, I would teach meditation to all the pregnant women I took care of. I would advise them to read books like the *Śrīmad Bhāgavatam* or other works on Vedānta during pregnancy because, as I explained to them, it would have an influence on their child. Many of my patients followed the advice. And when they were in labor, I would make it a point to be there with them for two or three hours before the actual delivery to reassure them. In the final stages of labor or before the anesthetist came, I would chant the *Viṣṇu Sahasranāma* or some other ślokas. This had a very beneficial effect on several patients. Some enrolled their children in Chinmaya Vidyalaya, others became members of the Mission, and yet others joined the Study Group.

Ravi Ravichandran, *Principal Scientific Liaison, U.S. Pharmacopeia, Rockville, Maryland, U.S.A.*

I was very unhappy and always afraid of being branded a 'failure.' During the nine years I worked in an organization, I never got a promotion. What made me feel worse was the fact that many of my colleagues made headway in their careers. The more anxious I became, the further away seemed that promotion. I was finally laid off from my job and moved to Maryland. There I started attending the talks at Chinmaya Mission for the first time. Guruji's lectures on *Gītā* chapters 3 and 4 made me realize that I was actually being pulled down by my own expectations. The study of *Bhaja Govindam,* in particular, in the Study Group made me realize how judgmental I was all the time about my colleagues and how I had such huge expectations of myself and them. Admitting a fault was not in my nature, and neither could I accept the faults of others. The consequences were terrible!

Study and reflection guided me to develop the attitude of accepting everyone for who they are and not for what they do. I put aside all my expectations and started doing the best I could under the prevailing circumstances. To my surprise, when I was not expecting it, a promotion fell into my lap. I have obviously made some headway, for I am now a successful member at my workplace.

Vivek Asrani, *Managing Director, Kaymo Fastener Company, Mumbai*

When I looked at companies that I admired like the Tatas and Infosys, I said to myself, "They are a forest, and, compared to them, I am a blade of grass. But I can be as green as they are." That was the starting point for how I wanted to build up the business. The regular exposure to the Study Group and constant interaction with my mother, who is the most dedicated Study Group sevikā I know, helped me gain clarity on what I wanted to do and how I would do it.

Since we spend the best years of our life and the best hours of the day at work, it was clear to me that it had to be qualitatively one of the best experiences. Then I sat back and thought, "What is the legacy that I want to leave for my children? Clearly, it is not just a bank balance. It is a character balance."

When I started this business fifteen years ago, it was highly import-dependent, and import duties were at eighty percent. Several people I discussed this with said that if I did not under-invoice, I had no chance of surviving in the business. So I said, "Then let's shut this down." I decided to build around this high cost factor of import duties, an environment, an ecosystem, a qualitative experience for my customer that he would be willing to pay for. As a result of that, we have never had to under-invoice.

On another occasion, when we were a very small company, we were negotiating a deal which could have doubled our business with one order. But we were dealing with one of the most corrupt purchasing departments of the private sector. I came back to the office and said, "We are not doing this." And, because we did not take that order, we went back and did other things: increased the product range, set up various business centers, and so on. Today, when I look back, I say, "Thank you Mr. Corrupt Purchase Officer for coming into my life, because had you not come, you would not have drawn out the creativity and innovation from within to build out the way we have done." But this only happened because we were committed to staying on a particular path, and doing things in an ethical and upright manner.

Jasmin Davidson, Principal Systems Engineer, Authentix, Dallas, Texas, U.S.A.

The effect of the Study Group was a kind of emotional maturation that allowed me to face human suffering. I work as an engineer and currently study social work. In the past, I was unable to face suffering because it consumed me. That's why I went into engineering. Now, I find myself able to offer help to others without being emotionally affected in a negative way. One may call this a kind of 'compassionate detachment.'

In my social work studies, I was sent out to a field internship, which included the supervision of guardianships of mentally incapacitated individuals. Currently, I am doing an internship with the police, assisting victims of violent crimes. These victims have all undergone traumatic experiences and their lives are often shattered. My duty consists of crisis counseling over the phone and at the police station, going out to crime scenes, hospitals, and so on, and, of course, there is a lot of paper work!

I know that I could not have done such work five years ago, and now I find myself doing it naturally and with joy. I have no doubt in my mind that attending the satsaṅga that is the Study Group and reflecting on the scriptures is what has made the difference. It has allowed me to be an efficient caregiver to those who need me at a time of a profound personal crisis.

XVIII

Influence of Study Group on Personal Life

Krishnan Kutty, Bangalore

Since my retirement, besides attending the Study Group, I have also been doing voluntary service in an institution for the blind. Once, I persuaded a young blind boy to come and attend a mini-yajña organized by our Study Group. At the end of that event, the boy wistfully commented that, had Gurudev's commentary been available in braille, he would have been able to read it. That remark touched me deeply, and, that same night, I resolved that I would try to make this possible for him since I knew braille.

With permission from Swami Brahmanandaji, I embarked on the project. It took us — my wife, my son, and myself — ten months to complete the work, 2,800 pages of braille in twenty-nine volumes. We produced five copies, and they were released by Swami Brahmanandaji. Subsequently, we made the *Gītā* in braille available in Kannada as well. But this time, the edition was without commentary.

Humcha Hari Prakasha, Frederick, Maryland, U.S.A.

The Study Group has helped me develop the ability to articulate Vedāntic concepts with clarity and confidence. During the first year of our Study Group in 2007, I attempted to explain Vedānta through the

BMI chart to an audience of faithful Christians at a Catholic Church. Overwhelmed by the occasion and overanxious to find the right words and flow, I fainted in front of them. However, recently, I was blessed with an opportunity to deliver a series of five lectures during the Sunday sessions on the topic "Concepts of Vedānta." I owe this change to our group leader, who compels us to talk in the Study Group class.

Leela Nambiar, *Chennai*

Unless you develop a love for the scriptures, you will not be involved in this study. Once you have a love for the subject, you will go deeply into it. And you will practice what you have read. Then only will you really know. You have to be a seeker to want to join the Study Group. These forty-five years of discussions have been a beautiful satsaṅga for me. Where else do you get such uplifting discussions? Only in Brahmaloka.

Sukeshi Sheth, *Mumbai*

In 2009, I was diagnosed with breast cancer. The one question I never asked was, "Why did it happen to me?" I said to myself, "OK it has happened and I have to deal with it." And while I was undergoing the treatment, there were two things that kept me going: (1) that I'm not the body and that all this is happening only to the body and not to me; and (2) that this, too, shall pass. And it *has* passed.

This attitude is the result of considerable thought and discussion in the Study Group. Another thing I have understood, thanks to the Study Group, is why I love trekking so much. I go to the Himalayas once or twice every year, and the reason I enjoy trekking there is because, while doing so, I have single-pointed attention — to get to where I am going. I am not disturbed by extraneous things, of thoughts about what's happening in Mumbai. I switch off because I know there is nothing I can do about it. I have understood that that is really living in the now.

Nirmal Bharwani, Singapore

From a social butterfly, I have morphed into a socially conscious person, doing more for society in the spiritual field. From being short-tempered, I have tempered myself down into a calmer and more effective person, practicing the principles of ṣaṭ-sampatti (six treasures, or disciplines, of the mind) as laid down by our scriptures. From giving importance to material things like jewelry and status, I have made my personality the jewels: my teeth are my pearls through my smile, my sparkling eyes are my diamonds which radiate love, and my strong convictions are my gold which shines through trials and tribulations.

K. P. Daswani, Hong Kong

In the beginning when I started conducting Study Groups, I became a little bit more egoistic than before. That is because people around you begin to respect you a lot more. Slowly, however, I realized, through deeper contemplation, that this definitely could not be the purpose of all this study. I asked myself whether I was evolving or devolving. Self-inquiry and self-testing became a passion with me. I wanted to test myself constantly to see whether I was capable of practicing the disciplines and various divine values that I spoke about so eloquently during study sessions.

Transformation happens, but it takes time and the Master's Grace. Once, I asked Gurudev, "Why do I fall?" And he said, "Just strive on. You don't have to leave these weaknesses; they will leave you."

P. G. Krishnan, Mumbai

I used to be very argumentative, very vociferous, and I would win every argument. But I have stopped arguing in the Study Group sessions because I saw that people were getting demotivated. They would skip my Study Group. Ultimately, their sādhanā was affected.

As a group coordinator and group member, it is my duty is to see that neither my sādhanā nor that of others is affected.

Aparna Durvasula, *Gaithersburg, Maryland, U.S.A.*

I find that I have an increased urge to share what I have with others. For example, after hearing Dr. Sadanandaji's narration of the *Gītā*, I donated $2,000 to the Mission without any hesitation. I had not donated a large sum like this ever before, and I was surprised at the ease with which I was able to part with the money.

Ritu Satsangi, *New Delhi*

Every time I have a setback and think that it is too much to handle, I come back to the Study Group and realize that these challenges are only there to make me stronger, and that all what is happening around me is not the goal of life. The group is like a loving and supportive family, each one encouraging the other when he or she is down.

Shruti Somani, *Mumbai*

Today, I can't have a conversation — whether it bores people to death or not — without Vedānta coming into it. It defines me. Take this away from my life and I don't know what I'd be. My husband went through a phase of being very resentful while I was trying desperately to explain my position to him. Then my sixteen-year-old daughter joined the CHYK Study Group. He saw the transformation in his daughter, but not in his wife! Now he wants to join a Study Group, too.

Deepak Verma, *Hamilton, Ontario, Canada*

Although I am younger than many in my group, I see them all as my equals, for we are all seeking answers to the same questions. The interactions in the Group have led to some meaningful discussions at home with my parents, sister, and close friends of how to approach the passing away of my brother. I believe I have helped them find comfort in knowing that it's not only okay to move on with their lives, but that it's required for the loved ones still here and for those that have passed away. I know it takes courage to approach loss and tragedy with a positive mind-set, but I also know it is the only way to honor life and the lives of those you love.

M. N. Malliswari, Hyderabad

Comparing myself with Study Group members helped me to understand that merely being good at communication only ensured that I was noticed, but it did not necessarily mean that I was more spiritually evolved than others. In fact the simplicity and humility of some of the members was, and continues to be, a source of great inspiration to me. I understood that these people were blessed because their simple life protected them from the agitations of a more materialistic lifestyle.

Gopika Kapoor, Mumbai

A few years ago, when my three-year-old son was diagnosed with a learning difficulty, the only thing that got me through each day was my Study Group and the knowledge that I had gained through it.

I realized how all that we talked about in our Study Group could and had to be applied in every day life — like dispassion, for example, which is so necessary. It is important to live with your child in the present moment and to remain completely focused. As a parent, you are the role model; so, how you perform is going to be observed by your child, and he or she will learn from you. You have to become mindful of everything you say and do. It was then that I wrote my first book called *Spiritual Parenting*. It was published in 2009 by Hay House, India, and was on the *India Today* best seller list. More than 8,000 copies have been sold. I feel this book just flowed through me. It was meant to be written, and I was chosen to write it.

Sumir Chaudhry, New Delhi

After many years of listening to texts being taught, it is only after joining a Study Group that actual study has begun. Slowly, the development of an inner awareness has gotten underway. The goal now is to make it continuous and strong so that it is not shaken under any circumstances.

Gina Gokaldas, Toronto, Ontario, Canada

Participation in the weekly Study Group not only demonstrated the value of taking time for personal reflection but also gave me an opportunity to make a conscious commitment to what is the most important thing in life to me: Self-discovery.

Pramila Raval, Bellaire, Texas, U.S.A.

I am so thankful that we have started to read two or three verses of the *Bhagavad-gītā* every night with all the family members, including my father and mother-in-law, via a conference call. I do not know if this experience would have been possible had I not maintained my commitment to the E-*Gītā* lessons. By dedicating myself to them, I have been able to create a family Study Group for the *Gītā*.

Vinita Asrani, Mumbai

After all these years, I have realized that study does give you a lot of clarity about yourself and about the world, but, at the end of the day, what really matters is His Grace. If we have to move forward in life toward our goal, we require His Grace. That comes with total surrender, dedication, and acceptance of His Will. The Study Group leads you to this realization.

XIX

Ācāryas as Catalysts

When he was just fifteen years old, Swami Advayananda joined the Study Group that his father attended. His deep fervor for this knowledge was further strengthened by exposure to Gurudev's talks and camps, thanks to his parents. Study Groups were conducted regularly at his home as well. Brahmacārī Sudhir Chaitanya (now Swami Dheerananda), Prof. C. G. Vasudevan, the late Brahmacārī Prasanna Chaitanya (later Swami Prasannatmananda), and Brahmacārī Shashwat Chaitanya (no longer with the Mission) were regular visitors to the house, and they conducted scriptural classes and held spiritual discussions four or five days every week. Swami Advayananda joined Sandeepany Mumbai after graduating from high school, the youngest ever entrant to the course. It is little wonder that when, as a brahmacārī, he was appointed head of Chinmaya Mission Kodaikanal, he laid much emphasis on the Study Group.

Swami Advayananda, *President, Chinmaya International Foundation, Veliyanad, Kerala.*

The Study Group was the prime activity that I promoted for nearly two years during my first posting as a young brahmacārī in Kodaikanal

(Tamil Nadu). Kodaikanal is a hilly area and a tourist resort in the summer. But basically, it is made up of several villages.

I started by setting up Study Groups in all the villages. We had to work in Tamil and the texts available were limited. We began with a short translation of questions and answers with Gurudev. I would go to a village, gather people together, and lead them in chanting a couple of bhajans. Then one person would be requested to read the Tamil text. Only a handful of villagers could read, but the others listened with attention, and all of them had their views on what was being discussed. I encouraged that and the Study Group got under way.

Then I introduced a study class notebook. The sevak would have to write the important points that had been discussed in the class. This was necessary because, as I started more and more classes in the different villages, I could not be present at all locations. So the Study Group notebook enabled me to keep track of what was going on in each class. It would be sent to me every week, and I would follow up with a telephone call to the Study Group sevak.

While in Kodaikanal (1993–96), I had to take charge of the center at Trichy as well, because the Ācārya there had been transferred. I found that the only way in which that center (Trichy) could remain active without an Ācārya was through Study Groups. I contacted all those who were interested and who had some prior experience in conducting both adult and Yuva Kendra Study Groups and gave them a brief training. Every month I set aside two days for such training. In this way, within four months, I had a good number of trained sevaks who were confident about starting a new group.

Before I launched these sevaks, we had a relay yajña on the *Bhaja Govindam* text. Each person selected one verse, did a thorough study of it, and then, on the appointed day, gave a discourse on it. Likewise, we had a relay yajña for the CHYKs as well. The audience was comprised of members of the Mission and the proud parents of CHYKs.

As the Study Groups got going (both in English and in Tamil), each group leader made it a point to train someone from the class who, in turn, would start a new class while continuing with the parent class. In that way some 20–25 classes started in Trichy within a year-and-a-half. Then, even while I was not there, Mission activity remained strong. Once the Study Groups became stronger, the Devi Group also began to grow. And with the Devi Group, the Bala Vihar became possible. So the Study Group is the means by which every aspect of the Mission can be strengthened and sustained. Things usually depend on the Ācārya and, when he or she is not there, they tend to slacken. That should not happen. The Mission work should never be dependent on one person.

As Ācārya of the Sandeepany course in Tamil/English in Coimbatore, I introduced *Art of Living* in Study Group format during the first month. There were some twenty brahmacārīs. They were divided into three groups, each with one moderator, and they would have a daily one-hour session of discussion. The idea was to make them think, to get them into the reflective mode before exposing them to discourses. It was also important to introduce them to the technique of gaining knowledge through discussion, as that is central to Vedānta.

Swami Swatmananda, Ācārya, CM South Mumbai

Swami Swatmananda was associated with Chinmaya Mission from the time he was born. His grandfather, Yashwant Tarkas, was a great devotee of Gurudev since the 1950s, and was leading five Study Groups when he passed away. Swami Swatmananda joined the CHYK Study Group during his first year in college and regularly attended the talks of Swami Mitrananda and other visiting Swamis at the Mission Center in Chennai. The experience of public speaking at a CHYK relay yajña inspired him to prepare talks on the *Gītā* every week. These would be presented at home to his parents, sister, and grandparents. In this way, spiritual knowledge remained an intrinsic part of family life. Soon thereafter, he decided to devote his life to the spread of this knowledge. He graduated from Sandeepany Mumbai in 2000 and, since then, has played a pivotal role in the development of Study Groups in South Mumbai.

Our vision is what Gurudev told us: The knowledge must spread to the maximum number of people. So we continue to expand our work by training a growing number of people in this knowledge and by encouraging them to create more and more Study Groups.

I have held regular classes specifically to train a growing body of sevikās to conduct Study Groups, Devi Groups, Yuva Kendra groups, and Bala Vihars. Over the years, we have completed a great part of the Vedānta course of Sandeepany. As the ladies learn and understand Gurudev's interpretation of Vedānta, the missionary spirit automatically comes to them. Through these classes, they get clarity and, thereby, confidence to take classes on their own and tackle the questions of group members. They gain exposure on how to open a particular topic and make it relevant to the current context, according to the age group they are dealing with.

When I first came here eleven years ago, we had just four sevikās. Today, we have more than twenty dedicated ones. Many of them are conducting Study Groups and pre-CHYK classes (age group 13–15 years). We have thirty Devi Groups in South Mumbai alone. I have told them that, by 2015, we must have a minimum of one hundred and fifty groups.

I visit these classes about once in every two months. The Devi Group has a plan for the whole year, which includes certain common programs for all the groups. These could be meditation workshops or a series of Hindu culture workshops. Since many of these ladies come from backgrounds where rituals are part of family life, I also teach them how to conduct certain rituals such as the *gāyatrī havana*, the *pādukā pūjā*, or the *Viṣṇu Sahasranāma arcanā*. That way, these practices acquire a deeper meaning for them, and they are able to enrich the religious life of their families.

We have introduced the curriculum for Bala Vihar, developed by Ācārya Darshanaben Nanavaty, in the Aditya Birla World Academy (a private school in Mumbai). These classes, known as Life Skill classes are held for grades one to eight. About twenty of our Devi Group sevikās conduct these weekly classes for grades one to six. Seventh and eighth grade classes are conducted by the Yuva Kendra members. So, in this way, the Devi Group, the CHYK Study Group, the Bala Vihar, and the pre-CHYK group are all very connected.

***Swamini Vimalananda**, Ācārya, CM Coimbatore, and Director, Chinmaya Vision Program*

Swamini Vimalananda was nineteen years old when she joined the CHYK Study Group. However, more than CHYK, it was the Vijñāna Mandir classes in Mumbai that really became her mainstay. It was a quest to seek the meaning of life, on a trip with a backpack, which eventually inspired her to join the Vedānta Course at Sandeepany Sadhanalaya, Mumbai. Her engagement with the Study Group began as a young brahmacāriṇī in Ahmedabad. Her formula for increasing all the grassroots activities, especially the Study Group and the Devi Group, is: 'Attend a class and take a class.' This is based on the scriptural instruction *svādhyāya-pravacanābhyāṁ na pramaditavyam*, do not neglect study and the spread of the knowledge.

The annual six-week Dharma Sevak Course held at Coimbatore (Tamil Nadu), is a very good forum to inspire seekers to join the Sandeepany Sadhanalaya, or to become sevaks of the Mission, especially for the grassroots activities. Weekly training sessions on how to conduct such activities and discussion groups are part of the course. They empower Dharma Sevaks to start and sustain Study Groups, Devi Groups, Yuva Kendra classes, and also the Bala Vihars. Graduates of the course have organized Study Groups in several cities in India and around the world.

The CCMT Education Cell guides all Chinmaya Vidyalayas and Chinmaya Colleges to conduct a weekly Study Group for teachers. However, the difference here lies in the fact that teachers do not come as seekers. They are primarily concerned with their professional and personal lives. So the texts selected for them are *Tips for Happy Living* and *Life of Vision*. Once they have been exposed to a few such simple but meaningful texts, their appetite is whetted and they become more receptive to some of the prescribed texts such as *Kindle Life* or *Tattva Bodhaḥ*. It is also recommended that they take the online Vedānta Course or the E-*Gītā* Course conducted by Chinmaya International Foundation (CIF).

Swami Sarveshananda, *Ācārya, Chinmaya Mission Dallas, and National Director of Chinmaya Mission Yuva Kendra (CHYK) West*

Before joining Sandeepany, Mumbai, Swami Sarveshananda distinguished himself as a Yuva Kendra member and was the founder/vice-president of the CHYK chapter in Serilingampally, a suburb of Hyderabad. Totally committed to developing the Study Group, he believes that, in an environment of constant time constraints, this forum acts like an energy capsule. During his first posting as Ācārya, Vijayawada (Andhra Pradesh), he managed about forty Bala Vihars, fourteen Devi Groups, and seven Study Groups. He also organized and inspired a large group of about 200–300 CHYKs.

When I first came to Dallas, I identified four distinct categories of people that I needed to focus on, apart from the Bala Vihar. The first was the youth group between 18–28 years, the CHYKs. The second was the DINKs — double income, no kids. These were young adults who were interested in Vedānta only if it catered to their specific needs and circumstances. The third was the Devi Group, usually stay-at-home moms. The fourth category comprised parents of Bala Vihar children. While the first three categories were genuinely interested in study and came on their own accord, the fourth category was there out of compulsion: parents who needed to be kept engaged while their children attended Bala Vihar classes. So the formats that I adopted for these various categories were naturally quite different.

What was common to the first three categories was a class of one-and-a-half hours duration with a text recommended in the Study Group syllabus. Members of these three groups would come to class having read and prepared a portion of the chapter assigned to them. They would have to present that portion individually in class. Thereafter, group members would be free to ask questions and seek further clarifications, examples, and so on, from the presenter. I would be the devil's advocate for the first few months. At the end of the session, when all presentations followed by questions and answers were over, I would speak for the last fifteen minutes.

After going through some of the preliminary texts, I took the more serious texts like *Bhaja Govindam*, *Upadeśa-sāra* or *Sādhanā Pañcakam*. A detailed and thorough discussion would be followed by a surprise test like the ones Gurudev gave us when we were in Yuva Kendra. The surprise lay in the śloka that they would draw by lot and then have to discourse upon in a relay yajña. The date for this yajña would be announced well in advance and many people would attend. After such a training, all the CHYKs, DINKs, and members of the Devi Group became fit to be Study Group moderators.

Meanwhile, I worked with the parents of Bala Vihar children in another way. Instead of a discourse, I engaged them in dialogue. While

I gave brief talks on the *Gītā* or another text every Sunday, they would be free to stop me and seek clarifications at any point. The format was informal, because I found that they would tune out with a formal lecture.

It took me about four years to get this group of parents to settle down. When they were ready, I divided them into Study Groups, about fifteen to a group. The moderators were selected from among the Devi Group and the DINKs. The CHYKs were encouraged to lead the senior students in the Bala Vihar classes. Currently, every Sunday, I speak to the parents of Bala Vihar children for half an hour, and then they disperse into their Study Groups and discuss what has been discoursed upon.

Ācārya Vivek, *CM Niagara Falls, Ontario, Canada*

In the past four years, Ācārya Vivek has given a phenomenal boost to the Study Group in North America, particularly, among young adults. Taking about sixty classes a month, and traveling incessantly to hold camps, retreats, talks, and Study Groups for all age groups, he has brought a new energy that is highly contagious. The response to his classes bears out the relevance and necessity of the Study Group format for drawing in educated and thinking young people. They are being groomed as the next generation of committed and dedicated leaders of the Mission.

CHYK West started in 2005. Today, it is a dynamic, organized body, poised to join hands with CHYKs around the world and play a global role in furthering the vision of Gurudev and Guruji.

The Study Group that I started in Mississauga, a suburb of Toronto, Ontario (the average age: thirty-five years), and the Study Group in Buffalo, New York (the average age: fifty-five years), have both completed their four-year mark. So, I am now weaning myself away from them. I visit them only once a month. Next year, my visits will be once in two months. It is like having a child who has grown up and can now manage on his or her own.

My aspiration for the Study Group is to create a love for the scriptures. Once the love is there, the Study Groups can be independent. As long as the love is not there, they need someone to guide them. I also emphasize that the moderator of the Group does not have to be the most knowledgeable person, but he or she has to be the most engaging. The moderator must facilitate through questions. You ask the right questions and you get the group members involved. You ask the wrong questions and you've lost them. That's why I keep using the phrase 'love for the scriptures.' The scriptures are a treasure house, and asking the right question is the means of opening the doorway. So, the moderator is the key to a successful Study Group.

We recruit new people to the Study Groups through word of mouth. There is no marketing. People get to hear of these discussions that are going on and about the happiness that participants have shown with their own smiles. So, there is both enjoyment and enlightenment — two important aspects of the Study Group. In short, word of mouth implies being an example of the personal transformation we talk about. If you live a more happy life, a balanced life, and a more inspired life, that's the strongest message you can give.

In Toronto we started with two people for the first month. I would drive for one hour and would meet with just one person. But then I would talk to people and he would talk to people, and now we have an email list of two hundred people. So, no marketing is done for any of the groups. It's simply, "You tell your friends if you have enjoyed it."

It is the Ācārya's role to make the Study Group members independent seekers. Gurudev often said, "I am not a mule Guru. I'm not going to carry anyone. I will show someone the way, but I will not carry them." That's effective leadership.

Whenever I hold a CHYK retreat, I emphasize to the participants that they should get involved in CHYK Discussion Groups. Similarly, when I do a jñāna yajña, I emphasize to those who attend that they should join the local Study Group. So the jñāna yajña is an instrument that should lead to the formation of Study Groups. As Guruji says, an event should evolve into a project, and a project should evolve into a movement. The event is the jñāna yajña, the Study Group is the project, and the movement is the daily svādhyāya. The ultimate goal of svādhyāya is liberation.

▲ *Śravaṇam*

▲ *Mananam*

◀ *Nididhyāsanam*

Multiple Voices: Collective Experiences

XX

Creating Communities

From Study Group to Center

The following narrative is just one of many, highlighting how a single individual has been the catalyst for creating a large community of seekers, eventually resulting in the formation of a Chinmaya Mission Center.

K. R. Pai (now Swami Ramananda) was a member of the first Study Group set up in Hubli, Karnataka. He recalls:

> In 1967, Dr. Sontake, an influential physician in Hubli, heard Gurudev's talks for the first time in Mumbai. Deeply impressed, he gathered a group of friends in Hubli and wrote to Gurudev inviting him to visit the city and hold a yajña.
>
> The organizers of this first visit, all men, had some initial apprehension. As a group of brahmins in a city largely

dominated by Vīra Śaivas,[11] they were not sure how much cooperation they would receive from the dominant community, and how much of a crowd they would be able to draw. The traditional rivalry and opposition between brahmins and Vīra Śaivas is well known. The Vīra Śaivas, over the centuries, have specialized in trade and commerce. They control not only the business in the city but also the many well-endowed religious and educational institutions. Another challenge for Dr. Sontake and his group was that the talks were going to be held in English in a predominantly Kannada-speaking area.

As it turned out, the attendance on the inaugural day of Gurudev's talk was way beyond our expectations. The hall where the evening talks on the *Gītā* were being held had a seating capacity of 2,500. And even on the very first day itself, the hall was full. The morning talks on *Bhaja Govindam* drew a smaller crowd — about 350–400 people, all professionals and businessmen. Much to our delight, invitations for bhikṣā started pouring in. Influential Vīra Śaivas, greatly impressed by Gurudev, came forward to invite him to their homes, to the schools and colleges run by them, and also to the Rotary Club.

As a result, during the valedictory function of the yajña, Dr. Sontake invited Gurudev for a second visit. Gurudev declared that he would accept only on the condition that Study Groups and Bala Vihars were started. He needed to be convinced that

---

[11] Vīra Śaivism was a protest movement in the twelfth century C.E. It opposed Vedic ritualism, the dominance of the brahmins, prejudices of the caste system, child marriage, and the prevailing form of Śaivism. Over the centuries, it gathered many followers, mainly from the large oppressed sections of society. The Vīra Śaivas distinguished themselves by the practice of wearing the Śiva liṅga around the neck as a mark of devotion and surrender to Lord Śiva. That is why they are also referred to as Liṅgayats. They are found mostly in Karnataka and a few parts of Andhra Pradesh.

people were genuinely interested and that they were willing to make the effort to sustain that interest.

Soon after Gurudev's departure, we organized the first Study Group. Fifty people joined, but slowly the numbers dropped to about fifteen members. Four were physicians, one was a Superintendent of Police, and the rest were businessmen. I was asked to be the facilitator. I remember how, often in the middle of the class, the patients of one or the other of our physician members would arrive and insist that the doctor come out of the class. That was because most people did not have telephones in those days. They would simply show up at the family doctor's house when there was an emergency. Finding that the doctor had gone to the Study Group, they would follow him there and ensure that they were able to meet him!

The first Study Group stood the test of time, and the dedication of its members grew. So, in early 1969, Chinmaya Mission Hubli was established. Dr. Sontake became the first President, and other members of the Study Group became the office bearers. We enrolled about 20 patrons and about 150–200 regular members. Since we had no premises of our own, all Chinmaya Mission correspondence, office material, books, and so on, were stored in my retail outlet.

Shortly thereafter, we invited Gurudev to visit Hubli for a second yajña. This time, we made it a point to include some influential Vīra Śaivas in the reception committee. The only way to ensure this was by insisting that the physicians in our group persuade their well-known and influential patients to join us.

Gurudev drew an even greater crowd during his second yajña. The outcome was two additional Study Groups and a wider circle of devotees and well-wishers of the Mission. The two sevaks of the new Study Groups became part of our committee, while members of the Study Group were also invited to all our meetings. Over the next few years, this committee then organized several yajñas conducted by the senior Swamis.

The first brahmacārī, Suresh Chaitanya (now Swami Poornaprajnananda), was posted to this center in 1980, eleven years after Chinmaya Mission Hubli was established. Our own Mission Center was inaugurated only in March 2002, thirty-two years after the creation of Chinmaya Mission Hubli. This long delay for a physical center was essentially because of a paucity of funds. It is only with the growth of Chinmaya Mission in Bangalore and other parts of Karnataka that those in a position to fund the center in Hubli realized that Vedānta, as a science of life, was truly beyond sectarian divisions and caste conflicts. The regular visits of Swami Brahmananda also played a pivotal role in this change of heart. He helped the Mission to grow, both numerically and financially, and removed the lingering doubts in the minds of the affluent members of society.

Spiritual Communities in Rural Areas

The rural development work of CORD (Chinmaya Organization for Rural Development) deals with all levels of society, from grassroots to policy level. It reaches out and empowers rural people through various community-based programs such as self-help groups, Mahila Mandals, adolescent girls' programs, a legal cell, a social justice cell, and so on.

Scriptural study and discussion is an integral part of the training for all those involved in these many programs. The term used for this study-discussion is svādhyāya. It is not structured the same way as the regular Study Group, nor does it follow a lengthy syllabus. In view of the many constraints in the rural context, group leaders must be creative, sensitive and adaptive to the constantly changing dynamics of rural community needs, temperaments, and abilities. As Dr. Kshama Metre, National Director for CORD, says:

> Although spiritual teaching happens everywhere, it is not uniform. Himachal Pradesh is emerging from poverty, so the villagers can focus more on the spiritual aspects of training.

Sidhbari 2012. Meeting of a Mahila Mandal in Sidhbari village, Himachal Pradesh. The chanting of bhajans precedes scriptural study and discussion on matters of local concern. The usual circular seating arrangement on this day was not possible because of heavy rain and lack of open space.

Sidhbari, 2012. Meeting of CORD workers during which there is always a short svādhyāya session taken by one of the workers (sitting on the stage with Dr. Kshama Metre).

> In Odisha where we have to take care of the basic needs of people, such as water, for example, satsaṅga among the people is minimal.

Kusum Mahajan, a volunteer Coordinator of some of the programs at CORD, describes the Study Group aspect of the special training programs organized at the CORD Training Center in Sidhbari. In her words:

> Grassroots workers from different states come periodically to receive training at the CORD Center in Sidhbari. The day begins at 7:00 A.M. with satsaṅga and svādhyāya. We start with meditation based on the *Art of Contemplation* by Gurudev, followed by one or two bhajans. This is followed by a discussion. In the case of village women who come for self-help training, I take simple texts like the Hindi translation of Swamini Vimalananda's *Why Do We*. I don't read from the

book. Instead, I begin by asking questions such as: "Why do you put a bindī on the forehead? Or, why do you do Namaste?"

This kindles interest and generates discussion. I also make it a point to explain to them the significance of the ślokas they chant everyday while they are here with us, such as the śloka from the *Gītā* that is chanted before meals. The idea is to give them a greater awareness of all that they do on a daily basis. At the end of the training session, they promise to conduct similar sessions in their own states with their own colleagues.

In the case of training for the Panchayati Raj program, the participants are generally mature and experienced people. I may then base the discussion on Guruji's *Hindu Culture.* Sometimes, we offer training to bank managers on how to deal with self-help groups. For them, I normally start with the topic of dharma. Often, through questions, the participants themselves lead the discussion to topics that are a source of concern to them. For example, once someone said, "I pray but my heart is not in it." That stimulates discussion. We have to be very flexible. These sessions are found to be extremely valuable and sometimes, on popular demand, we continue the discussion informally in the evening.

The hundred-odd field workers of CORD also have regular weekly meetings and a three-day session at the end of every month to report on field work and to plan for future programs. Svādhyāya forms part of these meetings. The purpose of this svādhyāya is to facilitate reflection and introspection on the extent to which work is carried out in the spirit of karma yoga as expounded in the scriptures. A test of this is the degree of happiness experienced by the worker and by the individuals whom the worker serves. Discussions are based on three texts: *Ātma Vikāsa Kī Nirdeśikā* (the Hindi translation of *A Manual of Self-Unfoldment*), Chapter 15 of the *Bhagavad-gītā*, and *Tattva Bodhaḥ*. Individuals are nominated beforehand to do a presentation and lead the discussion each time. Questions are then directed to the participants, and they are encouraged to relate the information to their personal lives.

Community in a War Zone

Vijay Kumar, a Study Group sevak from Washington, D.C., is an electronic engineer in the Department of Defense of the U.S. government. From June 2011–2012, he volunteered to serve in Afghanistan supporting the U.S. troops. While there, he started a Study Group for non-Hindus on the *Bhagavad-gītā*. He describes the experience as follows:

> It all began when I started attending the weekly Bible classes and scriptural classes for Jews that were being held regularly at the NATO military base in Kabul. One day, during the Bible class, I asked if there was anything offered on Hinduism. The chaplain replied that there was not, but if I wanted to start something, I could.
>
> I initiated the process, which, of course, entailed some red tape. My request went all the way up to military headquarters and the Defense Department in the U.S. I was required to give three references from Washington. One of these was provided by Swami Dheeranandaji, Resident Ācārya, Chinmaya Mission Washington Regional Center; the second, by Captain Pratima Dharam, who is the official Hindu Chaplain for the U.S. forces; and, the third, by Captain John Adams, U.S. Navy, Chaplain at Camp Eggers, Afghanistan. The whole process took about one month, and, at the end of it, I was appointed as a *Distinguished Faith Group Leader* (DFGL). The implication

of this post was that, if any Hindu who was part of the NATO forces in Afghanistan died in war, I would have to perform the last rites. It also implied that I could hold regular scriptural classes on Hinduism.

NATO TRAINING MISSION-AFGHANISTAN
COMBINED SECURITY TRANSITION COMMAND-AFGHANISTAN

OPERATION ENDURING FREEDOM

Certificate of Appreciation
is presented to

تقدیرنامه

Mr. Vijay Kumar

In appreciation of your outstanding leadership of the Hindu faith group at Camp Eggers. As an excellent representative of your faith and a vital member of the Camp Eggers community, your willing service and generous spirit contributed immeasurably to the morale and wellbeing of our Hindu personnel and are worthy of both our recognition and our deepest appreciation. Thank you for going beyond yourself to care for others in our command!

CDR Michael W. Gore
Command Chaplain
NTM-A/CSTC-A
Kabul Afghanistan

Signed:
27 May 2012

Staff Sergeant John Salazar
Chaplain Senior Enlisted Leader
NTM-A/CSTC-A
Kabul Afghanistan

I began with a Study Group on the *Bhagavad-gītā*. I spread word about the class through email and by word of mouth. What I made clear to everyone was that this was not a class to convert anyone to Hinduism. Ten people joined the class. They were Americans, British, some Africans and a couple of Indians. Most were Christians. There was one Muslim and one Jew. The classes were held every Sunday morning for an hour.

To begin with, I told the group members about Swami Chinmayananda, about Vedānta in general, and about Ādi Śaṅkara. They liked the concept of rebirth and reincarnation, but, of course, there were the inevitable questions, "How can you be so sure about rebirth? Is there any proof?" I tackled this question by describing an incident that had taken place during my last trip to India. One lady who had known me as a baby, mentioned, in the course of a conversation, that I had, as a baby, once peed on her. I was embarrassed and replied, "I don't remember!" To that she responded that just because I didn't remember did not mean that it had never happened.

In the same way, I explained that just because we don't remember our previous birth does not mean that it never was. There was logic in that. I then went on to say that if someone claims to be a doctor, we take it for granted that he went to medical school. Therefore, I emphasized, as I had heard Gurudev do so often, that if we are products of the past, it is certain that the future can be molded by the way we act in the present. This, too, gave them food for thought.

The subject matter that I covered was the first two chapters of the *Gītā*. I distributed Gurudev's *Holy Gītā* to the members of my class. The format of the class was discussion, teaching, and then questions and answers. I would ask everyone to read three ślokas and come prepared for a discussion. I also introduced group meditation at the beginning of the class. For most, this was their first exposure to Hinduism. They were fascinated by the story of the *Mahābhārata* and by the culture of India. An enthusiastic colleague, Karen Parker, volunteered to lead the guided meditation and became very good at it.

My work in Kabul provided me with firsthand experience of the hardships that deployed military and civilian personnel face. I volunteered to do counseling for people who were suffering from depression. This counseling was based on the *Bhagavad-gītā*. What I found was that, slowly, some of those I counseled also started coming to my *Gītā* class. The members in my class became friends and would often sit together in the dining hall or over a cup of coffee. Conversations often continued outside the class, whenever there was a spare moment. We became a little community within a larger community. I felt overwhelmed with gratitude toward Gurudev, for it was he who was working through me, drawing all these people toward this great life-transforming knowledge.

Kabul, 2012. Vijay Kumar with some members of the Gītā Study Group. Front row L to R: Kathleen Reiss, Vijay Kumar, Major Carolyn Bartley. Back row L to R: Richard Barfield, Col. Marissa Tanner, Theresa Sorenson, Col. Santosh Doddaman, Cdr. Alan Gore (Command Chaplain, Camp Eggers), Joe Scanion.

Community of the Chinmaya Family

The Study Group, if conducted according to the vision of Gurudev, ensures continual expansion of the Chinmaya Family community.

G. N. Seshadri's Study Group in Bengaluru has been meeting since 1984, and this has given rise to numerous new groups over the years. Below are highlighted the more recent developments over the last decade or so.

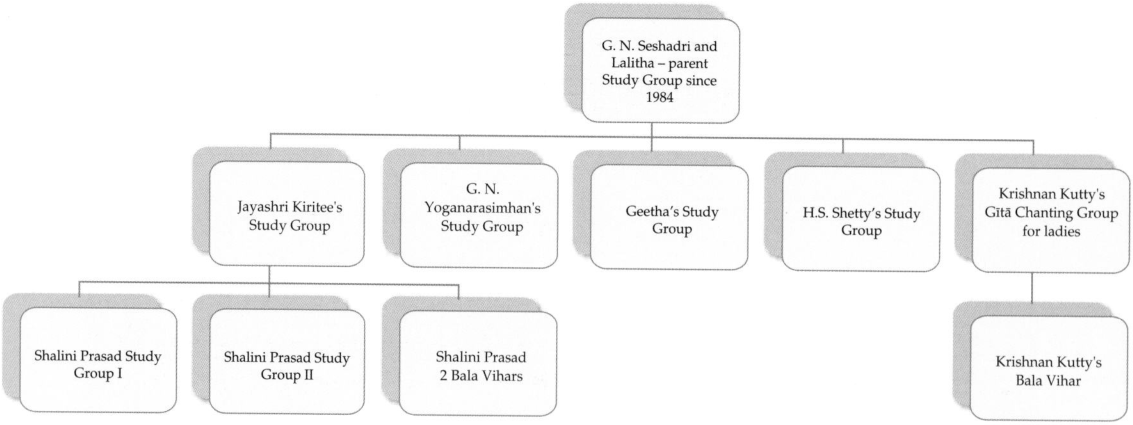

Off-shoots of G. N. Seshadri's Study Group in recent years.

The table above shows how, from a group of eight people meeting in one home, the Study Group has grown to include about sixty committed people meeting in six different homes for scriptural study (not counting the children involved in Bala Vihar). It also implies that at least fifty additional families benefit from this knowledge. All the groups mentioned above are independent, but their sevaks/sevikās continue to be part of the parent group. In that way, they continue simultaneously as group members and group leaders.

XXI

A New Role for Women

When social reformers in India agitated for the improvement of the condition of women in the nineteenth and twentieth centuries, they were concerned with issues such as the abolition of satī, child marriage, education for girls, and other discriminatory practices. Later, in the contemporary context, it expanded to issues such as the right to inheritance, the right to the same salary for the same work, and other such socioeconomic and sociocultural equality issues. What Gurudev did for women was to give them the right to spiritual knowledge and enabled their emancipation at the highest level. By making women the teachers and facilitators of scriptural knowledge, which had been the preserve of men for centuries, he empowered them to be active agents of change at the deepest and most lasting level.

A case study of the Devi Groups in Mumbai shows how the Study Group results in the empowerment of women in their personal lives, enabling them to take leadership roles in Mission activity. While we take the example of South Mumbai, the same holds true for much of Southeast and East Asia, where in Manila, Jakarta, Singapore, and Hong Kong, the domiciled Indian communities are essentially engaged in trade and mercantile activity. Men have little time for things other than their business, and the grassroots activities of the Mission are taken care of mainly by women.

South Mumbai is one of seven zones that form part of Chinmaya Mission Mumbai. It has about twenty-eight Devi Groups. Most of the women in the Devi Groups come from well-to-do families of the Marwari, Gujarati, and Sindhi business communities. Several live in joint families.

For the women in South Mumbai, freedom to join the Devi Group is not something that can be taken for granted. While the family has no objection to their socializing, there are invariably strong reservations when it comes to women's involvement with a spiritual organization. There is always the perception that a woman may be lost to the family, or that her priorities may change, leading to a disturbance in family life. Therefore, joining the Devi Group is a major step. Often, women join groups which have one or more women known to the family. One of the first things they do, thereafter, is to invite their in-laws and other family members to the festival celebrations at the Mission center. This is generally an experience enjoyed by all.

The husbands, who initially are reluctant to let their wives attend the Devi Group, invariably come to a stage of accepting this association. Gradually, there comes a stage when the wife can invite a swami home for bhikṣā. When this happens, then a satsaṅga takes place in the home. The husband will usually be present on this occasion. Once the ice has been broken, some husbands may agree, once in a while, to attend a talk.

At this point, Swami Swatmananda, Ācārya of South Mumbai, may offer some of the husbands certain responsibilities for a specific time-bound project like, for example, a corporate workshop. At one such workshop, Guruji was the principal speaker. The theme of the workshop was: LIVE FOREVER, RICHER AND RICHER. Several big names in the corporate world addressed the group. Such occasions enable the husbands to see that the Mission is associated with high-level professionals in every sphere of activity, including the business world. It is not just a religious organization, but one whose teachings have relevance to everyday life and work.

The Devi Group has resulted in strengthening the bonding between women of different generations within the family. It also ensures that the tradition of pūjās and rituals is kept alive for the next generation. Many who never understood the significance of the rituals that the family performed and who depended on pujārīs (priests) for pūjās are able today to conduct these rituals themselves. Their husbands view them with new respect.

The second outcome is that women have taken greater charge of Mission activities. Many of them have begun to conduct Bala Vihars and pre-CHYK Study Groups and to organize camps and yajñas. In fact, the Devi Groups have become a visible entity because of their considerable reach in the social circles of South Mumbai, because of the number of women involved, and the fact that most of them belong to large, extended families.

A third outcome is that they have brought a growing number of family members into Study Groups and into the Mission. Over the past fourteen years, Vinita Asrani, a seasoned sevikā, has drawn nine members of her extended family into one or the other of the five Study Groups that she facilitates. As she says:

> My own transformation has been tremendous. First of all, the Study Group gave me a focus in life. Secondly, it taught me to accept life as it is, for what it is. But, best of all, I became a source of inspiration to my family, particularly my children.

Young women elsewhere who have joined Devi Groups or Study Groups have described how this association has had a big impact on their parents and siblings. Natasha Chawla of London says:

> For a while I was the only member of my family involved in the Mission. Then my sister started conducting Bala Vihar classes and also began to attend a CHYK Study Group. Now

◀ *Sidhbari, 1991. Gurudev with Mona Mehra (L) and Vinita Asrani (R).*

slowly, my parents are coming into the Mission because they hear my sister and me talking of these things all the time. It is such a major part of our lives and my parents have seen how it has influenced us. So my dad joined a Study Group and has begun to read the *Gītā* regularly. Now, our conversations are nearly always about the *Gītā* or spiritual matters.

Parvathy Raman of Chennai recounts her experiences:

The group of women I gathered for my Study Group in 1996 all lived on the same street as I, here in Chennai. There were about fifteen of them, 30–65 years of age. All were housewives who spoke either Tamil or Telugu, so I had to use a mixture of English and the local languages. They were free in the mornings after 10 o'clock. Since they were fond of reciting the *Viṣṇu sahasranāma*, I started by teaching them the meaning of it. With the help of Śaṅkara bhāṣya (commentary of Ādi Śaṅkara) and Gurudev's commentary, I linked their daily experiences with the Advaitic truths, thus gently changing the direction of their thought flow.

To begin with, they were diffident, some of them with only basic literacy levels. Slowly, they learned to chant with correct pronunciation, to understand the concepts, and to apply them in their lives. They shared their experiences of trying to live what they had learned and it was inspiring for all of us. For example, if the husband or the children put them down as incapable of understanding or appreciating some technical point or intellectual concept, they would simply smile and say, "Yes, my brain is only capable of this much," because they learned to disassociate their BMI from their real Self. Remarks and sarcasm, which earlier had caused them deep hurt, were now brushed aside as they grew in self-confidence and inner strength.

The idea of titīkṣā (forbearance) appealed to them immensely, and they started practicing it with great enthusiasm. Discussions on the topic were characterized by considerable enthusiasm and wit as they learned to laugh at themselves. Gradually, these women, whose sole interest had been silk saris and jewelry, stopped going on incessant shopping sprees. From once a week, the classes became an everyday affair, six days a week for one and a half hours each day! Their dedication and devotion were quite amazing.

Next, I taught these ladies the *Lalitā Sahasranāma* with the meaning. Slowly, we progressed to other spiritual texts: the *Bhagavad-gītā*, *Tattva Bodhaḥ*, *Ātma Bodhaḥ*, the Upaniṣads, and *Vivekacūḍāmaṇi*. The *Praśna Upaniṣad* opened their eyes to the Sun God. When the sunlight streamed into their kitchen, they felt the Lord was blessing them by touching them with His rays. When the cooking was done, they remembered the fire that cooked and digested the food — *ahaṁ vaiśvānaro bhūtvā* from the *Gītā* (I am present in all beings in the form of digestive fire. *Gītā* XV:14) Those were days of intense spiritual sādhanā, and the teacher and the taught were both carried on wings of divine Grace.

The Devi Group training enables women to equip themselves with the wherewithal to promote tradition with wisdom and discrimination. It facilitates an understanding and appreciation of rituals that otherwise remain empty gestures. And it brings cohesiveness and strength to the family unit. By gaining an understanding of their culture, Indian women are playing an important role in raising the cultural standard in pockets of society. Slowly the effect will spread. That is the ultimate empowerment. By transforming themselves, members of the Devi Group have become catalysts for family, community, and societal transformation. They have become effective role models for their children and other women in their communities.

1960. Devi group members with Gurudev during the Akhil Bharatiya Chinmaya Devi Sammelan at Kollengode, Kerala.

▲ *1976. Gurudev addressing a Devi Group.*

Chennai, 1980. ▶ *Gurudev with Leela Nambiar (3rd from R), daughter-in-law Viji to her right, Lakshmi Reddy (standing second from L) and others who were part of Devi Groups.*

XXII

Vedānta in the West

When Gurudev Swami Chinmayananda reached out to non-Indians around the world, it was because he believed that Vedānta would give them a deeper understanding of their own faith, enabling them to live more fulfilling lives. Above all, Gurudev sought to give people the vision of oneness. Such a vision alone can usher in peace and harmony between different cultural, religious, and ethnic groups and ensure the wellbeing of this planet.

Numerous Westerners were drawn to Gurudev during his talks and yajñas. In the United States, they began to attend his yajñas in the mid-1960s and organized his visits and talks in various institutions. They started Study Groups, and the more dedicated of them became closely associated with his Mission. Nalini Browning, Rudite Emir, and Bill Sheldon were founding directors of Chinmaya Mission West. Richard Mullens, an attorney, was asked by Gurudev to form the organization SEVA, Inc., a precursor of CORD (Chinmaya Organization for Rural Development), in order to fund money for philanthropic purposes in India. In Switzerland, Adolf Bodel and Elizabeth Hallauer were responsible for hospitality to Gurudev whenever he visited that country in the 1970s and 80s. Thanks to them, many Europeans were introduced to Gurudev. All these individuals were part of the early Study Groups.

The majority of people whose lives were touched by Gurudev had had some prior exposure to other forms of Indian spirituality. In many cases, it was yoga, which eventually brought them to Vedānta. This was the case of Swamini Umananda of France and Swamini Amritananda of New Zealand. Others came because they were students of philosophy or psychology, and Vedānta offered them many new and meaningful perspectives on life. Ācārya Vilasini Balakrishnan of the Washington Regional Center was a student of philosophy at Tufts University when she first heard Gurudev. George Romney of Chinmaya Mission New York had studied philosophy, including Vedānta philosophy and psychology in Germany, while Aviva Keller of Switzerland was also a student of psychology and a practitioner of yoga.

Others were drawn to this knowledge because they were searching

▲
Boston, 1980s. Gurudev with Ācārya Vilasini.

for answers, which they could not find within their own faiths. As one Australian devotee of Gurudev puts it:

> Ironically, an outcome of hearing the great insights of Advaita Vedānta was that many of us began to understand the deeper, universal possibilities of the Christian teachings, perhaps for the first time. The personality and sayings of Jesus of Nazareth came alive and were imbued with new and subtle spiritual meaning. Outside the usual Christian theology, Christ's role as a God-realized spiritual master of that time and place — a 'son' of the Divine — now seemed self-evident. "I and the Father are one" became a declaration of pure Vedānta. Swamiji had opened our eyes to a universal vision of the Truth that included and then eclipsed all religious dogma. For most of us, it truly was a powerful and profound 'revelation.' It was a great gift, a pearl without a price.[12]

Brahmacāriṇī Arpita (Chinmaya Mission St. Augustine, Florida), who joined the first Study Group in Washington in 1978, and later went on to do the Vedānta course at Sandeepany Mumbai, describes how Vedānta and Gurudev revealed the true Christ to her in 1980:

> As I came into a room where devotees had just offered pādukā pūjā to Gurudev after his meal, my mind was stunned when I looked and saw the center of Gurudev's hands, feet, and forehead marked with the sacred *red* kuṅkum powder — in the exact places as Christ's wounds of crucifixion. It was the resurrected Christ sitting right before us!
>
> I suddenly realized how true this was: that even though Gurudev had not died *physically* — he had *spiritually* died to the body and mind long ago, having crucified his identification

[12] *Swami Chinmayananda: Master, Teacher, Friend — Remembrances from Down Under*, Chinmaya Mission Australia, 2006.

with them and been resurrected into the eternal Life of the Spirit, ascended to 'the Father in Heaven,' the pure infinite Consciousness!

◀ *Washington, D.C., 1989. Gurudev with Brni. Arpita.*

Vedānta in the U.S.A., Canada, Australia, and the U.K.

As more and more Indians joined Chinmaya Mission in the West from the 1980s onward, the Indian cultural aspect of festivals, pūjās, and other rituals became an intrinsic aspect of Mission life. In addition, the real emphasis in the Mission centers in these countries shifted to the Bala Vihar to satisfy the needs of expatriate Indians to raise children in an Indian culture and the Hindu religion. Therefore, for a number of Westerners, the perception grew that the Mission was an Indian religious organization.

Indian culture is not the priority of Western seekers. There are many who are interested in Indian music, languages, dance, and so on, and who are able to pursue these interests outside the Mission. The sincere seekers are interested only in the universal aspect of Advaita Vedānta, as was the case with those who became devotees or disciples of Gurudev. That continues to be the case even today with Westerners who are drawn to Vedānta; a genuine spiritual quest is still alive among many in the West, just as it was in Gurudev's time. Guruji's teachings are no different from those of Gurudev. What is different today is the profile of the Mission. As one CHYK Study Group leader from London puts it, "Presenting Vedānta in a universal way, yet being true to the Mission's Hindu identity, is a challenge when reaching out to Westerners."

The Hindu identity is indeed vital, because Gurudev's vision was, above all, to usher in a renaissance of Hinduism. As he said, his goal was to reconvert Hindus to Hinduism, and Hinduism includes culture and tradition (those aspects which Gurudev considered relevant in the modern age) as well as spirituality. Advaita Vedānta is the cream of Indian ethos and thought. It evolved in the Indian context and is associated with a specific outlook and mode of life. However, its core teaching is relevant for all mankind.

The cultural aspect of the Hindu way of life is necessary for national regeneration and to give Indians a knowledge of, and pride in, their heritage. Moreover, if India and Indians are transformed, a large section of the world's population will be transformed. They will become, in turn, catalysts for change at both the local and the global levels. Mahatma Gandhi's struggle for Indian independence through nonviolence (ahiṁsā), a traditional Indian value, inspired leaders around the world for decades after. Khan Abdul Ghafar Khan, Benigno Aquino, Martin Luther King, Jr., Nelson Mandela, and Aung San Suu Kyi are some of the well-known political leaders influenced by Gandhi. While the principle of nonviolence remained the same, each one of these leaders lived it out in the context of his or her own specific culture and environment.

Therefore, even if Chinmaya Mission has a Hindu identity, the knowledge it propagates is universal. It is available to anyone who seeks it. It is relevant in any and every context, and it will benefit every individual who sincerely strives to assimilate it. The Mission statement clearly affirms:

> *To provide to individuals, from any background, the wisdom of Vedānta and the practical means for spiritual growth and happiness, enabling them to become positive contributors to society.*

The Study Group is the ideal forum for the pursuit of knowledge in a culture-neutral context. Many of the early Study Groups in the U.S. and Australia had a mixture of Indian and Western members. Christine Grimmer of Melbourne, Australia, recalls the Study Group led by Dr. K. T. Ganapathy:

> Those were wonderful days and we relished the Study Group sessions for the insights they delivered. The mix of Eastern and Western worldviews, and perspectives from different faith backgrounds, made for interesting and lively discussion. At various stages, that first Study Group included Dutch, Polish, Italian, Indian, and Australian students. There were doctors, scientists, businessmen, journalists, teachers, university students, musicians, nurses, and folks on home duties among us. The age range was from 19 to 60-plus years.

Students of religion, psychology, and philosophy in the West appear to be most readily inclined toward classes on Vedānta. Mimi Robbins, who was part of the first Study Group in Boston, describes her encounter with Gurudev thus:

> It was the fall of 1971, and Swami Chinmayananda had come to Harvard University as the spokesperson for Hinduism on a conference for 'religions of the seventies.' I went, I listened, and I was spellbound. I felt I was hearing the best lecture on perceptual psychology I had ever heard. There was no dividing into categories of psychology, philosophy, or religion, but a united system of how we perceive and process experience.
>
> ...In early December, a yajña was to be held at Boston University, hosted by the Department of Religion. I rearranged

> my schedule and attended all ten talks on Chapter 12 of the *Bhagavad-gītā* on devotion. At the next-to-the-last talk, it was announced that one could visit the Swami at the motel the next afternoon. In spite of my fears and decision about not wanting to get involved with a Guru, I found my way to the motel. Swamiji greeted me warmly. I blurted out a question that expressed my doubts and confusion. His answer was: "Outer space seems intensely dark without any sign of light. Yet when an object enters into that space, it is illumined by the light to its full capacity to reflect and be seen." His answer resonated deeply. I felt filled with light and a profound peace.

Mary Cadden, a member of a Study Group in Maryland in 2012, has this to say:

> The *Bhagavad-gītā* is very important to me — so important that I've continued with our weekly Study Group for over ten years. I look forward to it because it nurtures me spiritually and is the only place I've found where I can sit, learn, and discuss the 'real' things that matter in life. Reading the scripture with a group of people who share values and strive to live in accordance with universal laws nourishes my soul. Reading and discussing the *Bhagavad-gītā* verses, parsing the words, considering their meaning in the light of day-to-day activities, and applying their lessons is often the highlight of my week.
>
> I am a Catholic born into a Catholic family. All of my formal education included studying my Catholic faith. Yet, the classes did not include the methodology of Vedānta. The *Bhagavad-gītā* Study Group uses the Vedānta method, which helped me to more deeply reflect on God and my beliefs about God. I now better understand my Catholic faith and know that

> God's laws are universal. As a result, I am comfortable with my Catholic roots and at ease with other faiths. I feel closer to God. The Study Group fostered a spiritual calling and gave me the courage to seek training as a pastoral counselor. It continues to support my life. For all of this, I am enormously grateful.

The Westerners who are part of a Chinmaya Study Group and who have recognized the value of the knowledge they gain through it can be the catalysts for drawing in more Westerners. Indian organizers of programs in the Mission centers invariably reach out, usually by word of mouth, to others within their own community. Since there are so many ready takers for what they offer, there is little incentive to look beyond their own community. Westerners, on the other hand, can be the best representatives of the knowledge and, through their own interactions, create interest in a wider group of people.

Piercy, California, late 1970s/early 1980s. Gurudev with late Imelda Rosenthal (seated) and Dorothy Brooks, both part of the early San Francisco Study Groups. Imelda participated in the first Chinmaya Lesson Course in Spanish conducted by Luis Jauregui.

San Francisco, 1971. Gurudev in discussion. Behind him (with beard) is Leo Graves who oversaw CM book distribution in the U.S.

Vedānta in Europe

In Zurich, Paris, and Vught (Holland), it is the natives of these countries who are leading Study Groups for their own compatriots. While Chinmaya Mission France was created in 1992 and has Chinmaya Shakti as its Center since 2004, in Switzerland and Holland, the Mission's activity is restricted to the Study Group. Very recently, in Romania, Daniela Badea has started three new Study Groups in Bucharest and Ploiesti.

What is common to all these countries is that virtually no Indians are involved with the Mission activity. It is evident that Indians overseas prefer an Indian cultural environment, which they do not find in a predominantly Western setup. This does not imply, however, that the Ācārya, too, must be Indian. Swamini Umananda has had an overwhelming response from the Indian community of all ages in London — a center that she visited regularly over two years in the absence of a local Ācārya. This can be explained by the fact that an Indian base of Gurudev's devotees existed in London before Swamini Umananda came on the scene. The already dedicated body of Indians appreciated the value of Sandeepany Sadhanalaya of Mumbai and the training it offers. They readily accepted an Ācārya trained and appointed by Gurudev. Where such a base of Indian devotees was absent, as in the case of Paris, the Indian community has kept its distance. The center in Paris has not been able to draw Indian members in any significant number.

Swamini Umananda, however, has been able to expand her outreach to the Western audience, not only in France but also in French-speaking Canada and other parts of Europe. Aviva Keller of Switzerland and Paula Spronk of Holland, both graduates of Sandeepany, Mumbai, have managed to sustain the flame kindled in their own hearts by Gurudev and ignite it in those of a small group of people around them.

It is unrealistic to expect large numbers of Westerners to be associated with Chinmaya Study Groups. It is only the serious seeker of knowledge who will remain with a Study Group for any extended period of time. Even among Indians, those who join the Study Group are much fewer than those who attend talks and yajñas and serve in other aspects of Mission work. Moreover, even in Gurudev's time the number of Westerners who actually remained faithful to his Mission and to the Vedāntic teaching he expounded were few, but the commitment of these devotees has been exemplary.

Chinmaya Mission Centers for Westerners

The running of Chinmaya Shakti in Paris, over the past twenty years, has borne out that centers, where the audience is Western, will inevitably be distinct from those run by Indians and for Indians. In Paris, membership is entirely French, and has remained at about forty to fifty members in the past twenty years. Indian philosophy creates an undeniable interest in France. Therefore, in all these years, Chinmaya Mission France (CMF) has touched a good number of sincere seekers and has always worked with the help of a dedicated team. There are, however, challenges in the development of Chinmaya Mission in France, summed up by Swamini Umananda:

- The most popular discipline is haṭha yoga, which is not always practiced in a spiritual way. The scriptures do not attract as much interest as haṭha yoga does.
- When people in France see the words 'philosophy' or 'study of the scriptures,' most of them think it to be an intellectual approach. So most of the newcomers to CMF are fascinated by the vision of Vedānta, but are not really interested in the practice. After two or three years, they think they know Vedānta and they leave. In that case, there is no real appreciation of the teaching and no real attempt to transform oneself.
- As for the seekers wishing to progress spiritually, the majority is not ready to put in the effort. They are very attracted by masters whom they see as 'saviors.'
- The modern mentality is also very reluctant about commitment at every level. Even at the spiritual level, people usually find it difficult to commit to one path, one Guru, or one center. Most of our members belong to other organizations as well, and they are committed to none of them.
- Very few members engage themselves in sevā, which is the fruit of love, spiritual practice, the desire to change, and commitment.

For all these reasons, Chinmaya Mission France has redefined its priorities for the future. While the grassroots activity of the Study Group and classes will continue at the center, the growth will probably come more from the outreach talks given by the Ācārya in other spiritual centers. In addition, the publications will continue because they sell

London, 2012. Swamini Umananda visiting a Study Group. Seated on the floor L to R – Jayasri Pillai, Irene O'Connor, Aruna Bhalla. Kneeling on the left – Rupa Das, Ayush Nawbatt, and behind her Lal Nawbatt and Mannu Bhalla (standing). Smita Samani next to Swaminiji, Chitra Balasingham (kneeling), and Zia Rawji on the right.

well. The initial French translation of Chinmaya Mission books was undertaken specifically for the purpose of the Study Groups' needs and for regular classes. Swamini Umananda also feels that e-books and the online teaching of courses specially developed for a French-speaking audience are good ways to spread the knowledge.

Aviva Keller describes the evolution of Mission activity in Zurich thus:

> In Switzerland, the term 'mission' has negative connotations because of the role of certain Christian missionary sects that

> have not always been viewed with a positive eye. ... Moreover, the church is still very much alive in this country — both Catholic and Protestant. People always go there as children and are culturally rooted in it. And so I always felt reluctant — as have other people — to be like missionaries of a religion. We think that the universal aspect of Vedānta would help Europeans.

Paula Spronk feels that she must take Gurudev's Vedānta to the Dutch people in the following ways:

- First, by living His Vision within our family life and in that way to show Vedānta practiced in daily life;
- By inviting people to our home for concerts, music workshops, and so on, so that they can have a taste of the spiritual atmosphere here at home;
- The ones with a spiritual inclination are invited, one step further, to personal meetings, the Study Group, to attend Guruji's yajña, and to satsaṅgas in our home.

Truus van der Meer, who has attended Paula Spronk's Study Group in Holland, says:

> In April 2003, I started the study of Vedānta with Paula Spronk. She first introduced me to the philosophy of Vedānta by reading some articles and chapters from some books. First, I studied alone with Paula; later, another woman joined the two us, but she left after some time. The two of us continued. ... It took time for me, a Westerner, to get used to the Indian habits and presentation. After about two years, I was struggling with the question: Is this my path? Is it not elite and egocentric? So I took a break. But I returned to Paula, and she gave me a warm welcome to continue studying with her. She is an example for me.
>
> Swami Tejomayananda was the very first Indian I met at

> the camp in France in 2009. I was very inspired by his lectures, and I was glad to be there. The Indian way was not familiar to me, so it took time to get accustomed to the chanting of the mantras, for instance, in Sanskrit. I do realize now that the text we studied in France about death (*Kaṭha Upaniṣad*) helped me to get over the loss of my husband last October (in 2012). So it makes more sense now.

Daniela Badea received guidance on how to conduct the Study Group during the Dharma Sevak Course. However, the experience of actually starting such groups in Romania[13] has been quite different. She admits, "It is better to be able to improvise according to the situation, while keeping in mind the scope and dignity of the Mission."

While some people have been drawn to Daniela's Study Group out of curiosity, others have come with open minds, and yet others have been hostile. In Romania, after forty years of communism, anything that is perceived as the cult of a personality is viewed with misgivings. Moreover, the church, muzzled during the Communist regime, is quick to extinguish any 'spiritual pollution' in its efforts to establish a resurgent Christianity.

Rudite Emir of Los Altos, California, gave talks on Vedānta and held spiritual camps in her native Latvia for about fifteen years, starting one year after Gurudev's Mahāsamādhi, but not under the auspices of the Mission. As she explains:

> I felt that Latvians needed to hear this knowledge in their own language and in their own cultural context. After my first

[13] Vedānta was introduced to the intellectuals in Romania about a century ago by Mihai Eminescu. Not only did he write the first Sanskrit Grammar book, but he also compiled some poems that are completely Advaita Vedānta in thought and expression. Other scholars who have translated, or written about, Indian philosophy in Romania are Sergiu Al George, Mircea Eliade, and Amita Bhose.

Vedānta talks in Latvia in 1994 (which were sponsored by a local organization), I realized that the people most drawn to the spiritual life there were also closely aligned with Latvia's ancient pre-Christian culture, which was replete with deep spiritual meaning. Once I discovered that wealth and the early literature that was so spiritually rich (songs and verses called *dainas*), I tied my talks of Vedānta into that tradition to show the unity and universality of spiritual thought. I thought the Latvians would understand the Vedāntic teaching more readily that way rather than in the context of Hindu culture. There were many opportunities to show the parallels between Vedānta and the ancient *dainas* of Latvia.

Latvia, early 1990s, Rudite Emir with BMI chart translated into the Latvian language.

The Study Group seems the best option for sustaining the study of Vedānta in small informal groups. The sharing by Western sevaks of their personal experiences with the Guru and of their studying at Sandeepany Sadhanalaya is of as much importance as the study of a prescribed syllabus. It is this sharing that makes the knowledge more accessible. It brings the Guru and a tradition alive in the minds of people who are culturally and physically removed from it. Moreover, these householder disciples of Gurudev are visible examples of how people can live normal lives at the professional, social, and cultural levels and yet be steeped in this knowledge and the attitudes it implies.

Conclusion

Gurudev sought to make people devotees of knowledge. Today,

Guruji's talks have as profound an impact on his Western listeners as Gurudev had on his. It is these Westerners who must take the initiative to form Study Groups. Or, Westerners can enroll in the E-Vedānta or E-*Gītā* courses that are available online and begin a more sustained engagement with Advaita Vedānta. Where possible, they can attend the classes of the local Ācārya. Through love for this knowledge, some of these seekers will develop a love for the Guru-śiṣya-paramparā and for the tradition in which it has been nurtured.

The third generation of Indian and second generation of Western members of the Chinmaya Family in the West will inevitably play a growing role in bridging the cultural divide. Jasmin Davidson of Dallas sums it up most aptly when she says:

> The Chinmaya Study Group is an important and relevant forum in today's world, because the world has become a global village and we all share a common fate. The time has come to share spiritual teachings with others. As much progress as humanity has made on one hand, we have also brought upon ourselves terrible crises. Those among us who can should step up to the plate. On the wall of one of my social work classrooms, there is a quote by Margaret Mead that says, "Never doubt that a small group of thoughtful, committed citizens can change the world. Indeed, it is the only thing that ever has."

Chinmaya Mission can make a difference in this world, and past experience has shown that the Chinmaya Mission Study Group can be a vital agent of change.

Sidhbari, 1983. Responding to the numerous letters that arrived daily from devotees around the world.

Views, Recollections, and Reflections

XXIII

Gurudev Answers

Gurudev's letters of guidance to numerous Study Group sevaks are a treasure in themselves. Here are a few samples of this rich teaching of Advaita Vedānta, personalized and profound, from the collection of Ajit Sukhatankar who has been a Study Group sevak for many years. Gurudev writes:

> Such questions as your group has raised are natural in the bosom of the early students who are just entering into the Hall of Wisdom. When your studies mature, you learn to smile at your own initial doubts. This should not make you disappointed or shy. Questions, you must ask. All that I want you to understand is only that when the questions are arising in your mind, you shouldn't despair but discuss them as best as you can and let the group sevak note these questions down in a notebook. Once a month the questions that were not correctly or satisfactorily answered may be read out in the class, and all of you shall then realize that, in the light of what you have already studied, many of the questions that

you had in the past stand completely cleared. Therefore, the study classes must strictly follow the scheme of study that has been advised — and found to be efficiently useful in all the branches of the Chinmaya Mission both within the country and around the world.

Your Questions

Q. *In which part of the body does the Spirit or Soul reside? Has it any size, etc?* (The *Kaṭha Upaniṣad* states that the soul is the size of the thumb and resides in the heart.)

A. The students of the Study Group must clearly understand that they should not use the word 'soul,' but must always use the word 'Ātman,' or the 'Self.' The 'Soul' of Christianity is not the Ātman of the precise science of Vedānta. To the Christians, there is a good soul and a bad soul. They seem to confuse Soul with sole! Soul, therefore, means only the *jīva*, the PFT (Perceiver, Feeler, Thinker). Ātman, the Self, is OM, the Reality.

That which is conditioned alone can have a shape; that which has a shape has got properties; and that which has got properties must necessarily perish. The Ātman is Immortal, Imperishable, Immutable. Therefore, it cannot have any shape — It is All-pervading.

Where does your Consciousness remain in the body? Supposing a man is put in an uncomfortable position with his head in the refrigerator, feet in the oven, his wife beating him on the bottom, and his children needling him all over — will he not be conscious of the coldness of the fridge, the heat of the oven, the agony of the beating, and the sorrows of the needling? Consciousness is within, without, everywhere. In a medium of Consciousness, you exist and your equipments function.

It is like a pot on the table in a room. The space is within the pot and outside the pot. If you ask me where exactly in the pot is the space, you are asking me the question that you have raised!

In the *Kaṭha Upaniṣad*, no doubt, there is the reference to what you have mentioned. This is for the purposes of early meditation (upāsanā) for the students. It is exactly like we recognize Śiva in the Śivaliṅga, Christ on the Cross, and *Khudā* in the direction of Mecca. The National Flag represents the nation, but the flag is not the size of the nation. The thumb is not the size of the Self.

Q. *What is the real difference between intellect and mind, brain and heart? What are their respective functions?*

A. Because this is the very first time you have asked me questions, I am elaborately replying. The mind receives the stimuli from the world outside and presents them all to the intellect for rational assessment and final judgment. The mind is *saṁśayātmika*, of the nature of doubt. The intellect is *niścayātmika*, of the nature of discrimination and judgment. Thus, so long as you have a doubt — should I or should I not, can I or can I not, is this Ramu or Kittu — it is the mind. When the same, in the light of more data and deeper analysis, has come to a judgment — I will go, I will do it, certainly this is Ramu — it is the intellect. Thus, thoughts in a state of flux, agitated with doubts, together constitute the mind, the receiving instrument. And the peaceful state of thoughts in final judgment and satisfactory assessment of a problem, 'solidify,' as it were, into a knowledge, a determination, a willing — such states constitute the intellect.

Just as there is a bulb and the light, the heater and the heat, so, too, we have the intellect and intelligence. Intellect is the equipment; intelligence is the light of understanding that comes to beam out of it. The equipment of the intellect in the gross physical body is the grey and white matter in the cranium called by biologists as the 'brain.'

Heart is not the pumping bloody organ that centralizes all the activities of the circulatory system. 'Heart' here is not used in the language of the biologist, but in the language of the man of literature. When we say, "He is a man of heart," or "a man with a large heart," or "the heart of the problem," or "my heart is broken," or "I have no heart in this work" — what do we mean by 'heart' here? In spiritual literature, when we use the word 'heart,' it means 'the core of the personality.' The essential individual in us is the heart.

I recommend that the Study Group members strictly follow the study scheme. Then, such doubts will resolve themselves, maximum in six months' time.

EXCERPTS OF LETTERS FROM GURUDEV

JANUARY 17, 1980, BAHRAIN – TO SOM PRAKASH OBEROI, KUWAIT

You have grown up and deepened. Congratulations. Continue your own studies, reflections, and serving others. It is only when you discuss with others that your own understanding gathers a serious and gracious depth.

SEPTEMBER 12, 1987, DURBAN – TO THE GĪTĀ STUDY GROUP LED BY JYOTI M. KUNDALIA, SINGAPORE

Of all the bhikṣās, yours has been the most satisfying, because it was offered by hearts soaked in *Gītā*-prem. Thank you. Kannaiya has fully succeeded in imparting the *Gītā* message into your hearts.

MAY 30, 1990, TOKYO – TO JYOTI M. KUNDALIA, SINGAPORE

Discover among people known to you who are equally interested in spiritual satsaṅga, and bring them all together into a group and may you work at it together. It is indeed more effective in the early stages.

Be regular in your reading of *Kaṭha* and *Gītā* III. Be sincere. Be regular. These are the secrets of spiritual unfoldment.

In 1966, Dr. A. K. Shah of Ahmedabad wrote the following question to Gurudev[14]:

Q: *What will our Study Groups do except fatten the Bhasmāsura?*[15]

A: This is exactly what I want. The Bhasmāsura running after Śiva is an intelligent aspirant rushing forth to the Satsang Halls. Let them struggle hard with their intellect to contact the Lord and, in the process, they shall turn their investigation into themselves and end in their Self-discovery. What exactly is wrong in it? This is the great grand path of jñāna. Listening to the teachers, reflecting upon them are the preparations without which meditation becomes only a delusory pose assumed by spiritual egoists.

If the Study Group program is wrong, then you are criticizing the declaration of Ācāryas like Vidyaranya Swamigal who, in *Pañcadaśi*, declares:

tat cintanaṁ tat kathanam,
anyonayaṁ tat prabodhanam

Thinking of it (reflection); reading it; mutual discussion — giving it out — are the very processes of Brahma Vidyā. If you are not familiar with the stanza, please consult your Ācārya.

I hope you will join the Chinmaya Study Group in Ahmedabad and, with your experience and wisdom, guide and lead the new youngsters who have discovered a novel joy in śāstra study.

---

[14] *Tapovan Prasad*, July 1966.

[15] Bhasmāsura was an asura who gained from Lord Śiva the boon that anything he touched would turn to ashes. He began chasing Lord Śiva himself, and finally was tricked by Lord Viṣṇu to touch his own head and be reduced to ashes!

Sidhbari, 1990. Gurudev with Dr. AppaRao Mukkamala

Dr. AppaRao Mukkamala, who has been part of a Study Group since 1978 in Flint, Michigan, recalls:

> In the *Nārada Bhakti Sūtra*, one of the verses (v. 65) states that you should convert the six negative emotions — desire, anger, delusion, miserliness, arrogance, and jealousy — into positive ones. I wrote to Gurudev and asked how that was possible when the emotions in question are so inherently negative. Gurudev wrote back and said:
>
> "All the six 'families' of thoughts can be turned subjectively upon ourselves or upon Him. When these thought impulses are turned outward, upon, and toward things, then they become forces of dissipation, occasions to exhaust our mental vitality; but when they are turned toward yourself or the Lord, subjectively, they all become creative and totally integrating forces.
>
> "Thus, when lust is turned toward Him, it becomes Meera-like supreme devotion. Anger, too, when directed at the Lord becomes an expression of extreme devotion (just as your wife becomes angry with you). Jealousy of other seekers who are progressing, he can become more and more sincere in putting

forth effort in the right direction. Miserliness (lobha) refers to compromising with our values not even an iota, and like a miser looks after his wealth, the seeker looks after his spiritual perfection; vanity (madā) that 'I am a devotee and, therefore, I should not live mere animal values.'

"Thus, if you start practicing and applying all of them upon yourself instead of upon others, the so-called negative tendencies become aggressively positive."

One time when Gurudev was visiting our home to meet with our Study Group members, he started out the discussions by saying, "OK, shoot! What questions do you have for me?"

Somebody asked, "Swamiji, could you explain Māyā?"

His answer, accompanied by a cascade of merry laughter, was: "You wait all this time for the Guru to come and all you want to know is: What is that which is not!!"

Rudite Emir

We would start a Study Group with fourteen or fifteen people, and then the numbers would come down to five, four, three. Then I would get discouraged and write to Gurudev. He wrote back, "The minimum required for a Study Group is two. Unless it comes down to less than that, don't stop. After all," he emphasized, "this is your own sādhanā. It was one Vivekananda that shook the entire world. Probably one of these two in your group is a potential Vivekananda who can shake Bangalore. Don't stop."

K. G. B. Gupta

Training the disciple to live and further the vision of the Master.

The perfected disciple becomes the Master.

XXIV

Guidance from Guruji

A few Study Group sevaks met Pūjya Guruji Swami Tejomayananda on November 11, 1999, at Sandeepany Sadhanalaya, Mumbai, for guidance on the Study Group activity.[16] Here are some excerpts:

Q. *Swamiji, why is it that Study Groups face the problem of a lack of sevaks and dwindling attendance?*

A. Low numbers in the Study Groups need not deter us, because, even in worldly activities, the number of people working sincerely is always less. The objective of the Study Group should be very clear to all its members. Without this, there cannot be any commitment among sevaks or members, and the problem of dwindling attendance would continue.

The purpose of life is Self-realization, and, therefore, all our activities should be toward that goal. On this path, yajñas (śravaṇam) give us the vision of the śāstras. The Study Group is a forum for mananam (reflection) and the digestion of ideas, so that our knowledge is free of doubts. Spiritual health is as important as physical health. Just as a hospital helps us to regain physical health, so, also, does spiritual study enable us to regain spiritual health. It is the responsibility of each

---

[16] Downloaded from the net where it was originally posted by Ram Chandran on April 14, 2000.

member of the group to make the discussion fruitful and interesting by regular study.

As far as sevaks are concerned, there is a fear in their minds that they do not know enough. This results in members hesitating to become sevaks. The latter must have an attitude and readiness to share the benefits that they have gained, with other members of the Study Group. A positive attitude will give maximum benefit to the sevaks. In case of unresolved doubts or questions, the groups could write them down and get them clarified once in a while by the Ācāryas of Chinmaya Mission.

Q. *What is it that would attract people to the Study Group?*

A. Two things attract people to the Study Group:

1) If their needs in life are fulfilled; and
2) If their interests are fulfilled.

In life, one sees that a highly spiritual person has minimum material needs, while a highly materialistic person has minimum spiritual needs. Then, you have some people who feel the need, but are unable to sustain their interest because their expectations are too high.

Q. *What factors would you name as responsible for the spiritual learning process to take place?*

A. Four factors, each as important as the other, make the learning process complete: 25 percent the Guru's blessings; 25 percent self-study; 25 percent group study; and 25 percent the time factor.

Q. *How do we go about studying the text in the class?*

A. Every text has a central theme around which it revolves. Look for this first. Each verse should be taken up in the following sequence: first, the word meaning; then the translation of the entire verse followed by the commentary; and, finally, the sum and substance of the verse.

Q. *Could you suggest a few ways to make the discussion interesting?*

A. The applicability of the knowledge gained through study to daily life should be stressed. Use real life examples for this. Second, you may ask the members to express their understanding in their own way. For example, someone interested in poetry could write the theme of the verse in poetry form; an artist could depict it in picture form; a musician could tune the verse in some *rāga* (musical melody); a grammarian could explain the Sanskrit grammar. You could also have a quiz, 'fill in the blanks' or 'complete the verse' contests to keep up the interest of the members.

Following is an excerpt from a talk given by Guruji during the Study Group Sevak Training Program held at Chinmaya Vibhooti, Kolwan, September 8–12, 2009:

> A lack of knowledge of what the Study Group represents invariably gives rise to wrong expectations. Often, people join a class after having attended a jñāna yajña, which they found very enlightening and very powerful. Inspired by the experience, they come to the class expecting to listen to the same kind of discourse. So, of course, they are disappointed. Here, one has to make the effort to read, to study, and to think. Moreover, the *sevak/sevikā* who runs the study class may not be as eloquent as the Swami.
>
> We all either have a particular level of expectation, or we tend to compare ourselves with other people. It is as though I were to go to the gym for one month and then compare myself to Dara Singh, the wrestler, whose whole life has been devoted to bodybuilding. Or, it is like me going to an āśrama for ten days or two weeks and then comparing myself to Bhagavan Ramana Maharshi. In that case, I will certainly not perceive any change in myself. When you compare your present thinking

with what it was some years ago, then I am sure you will notice a difference. This transformation is a gradual process, and, if you have gained something, then it is inevitable that it will express itself in your life. The pace of change may vary but change will be there.

Nirmala Limaye of Washington, D.C., once asked Guruji: "Do you think we should do anything differently in our Study Group?"

Guruji asked just one single question: "Is everybody enjoying it?"

"Yes", replied Nirmala.

"Then continue what you are doing."

XXV

Ācāryas' Views

Gurudev established the Study Group for lay seekers and the Sandeepany Sadhanalayas for those wanting to engage in full time study. However, the need for group discussion and interaction is equally important for both the gṛhastha and the sannyāsī. Below are some examples of how Swamis of the Mission have occasionally used the Study Group format for their own study and reflection. Other narratives talk of the challenges Ācāryas face in establishing Study Groups, or of their successful experiences in promoting this forum.

Swami Viviktananda, Regional Head, Kerala

Ācāryas need to have discussion sessions periodically. When we speak from the platform to the general public, we have to simplify the subject and express things in a manner that is comprehensible to the average person. If we go deep into the subject, people invariably lose interest. But, as Ācāryas, our roots are in the śāstras and we need to be thorough in our knowledge of them. Since we cannot have such a level of discussion with the public, we need to have it among ourselves. Secondly, when we speak to the public, it is *pravacana*. But *svādhyāya*, too, is very necessary. Svādhyāya and pravacana must go together. Moreover, in the field, the scope to improve our Sanskrit, the language in which the śāstras are written, is very limited. We have to attend to so many other things. So such sessions are needed for our own growth.

With this in mind, about three years ago, we organized an *Ācārya śāstra sadas* at CIF for the Ācāryas of Kerala, under the guidance of Swami Advayananda who is a great scholar. We would meet every four or five months for an intensive three-day session. We took up the first four verses of the *Brahma Sūtras* (*catursūtri*) for an in-depth study, along with *Śaṅkara bhāṣya* and annotations. Each day, we had five sessions, each for an hour and a half. During the first *Ācārya śāstra sadas*, all three days were devoted to a study of the *adhyāsa bhāṣya,* which is Śaṅkara's introduction to his commentary.

The second time we met, four months later, we took up the first sūtra of the *Brahma Sūtra*. That alone took three days to cover, for it is an extremely profound topic. We focused on the bhāṣya, but, where necessary, Swami Advayananda would read the *ṭīkā* as well. While the text is entirely in Sanskrit, our interactions were in English. Swami Advayananda facilitates the group. He is the one who structures the sessions, who offers explanations, and who stimulates discussion. The rest of us listen, and each time he raises an issue, we discuss it. He ensures that all doubts are cleared before proceeding to the next word, or next line of the śloka.

In this way, we have had four or five *śāstra sadas* for the *catursūtri* alone, each session lasting three days. Thereafter, we decided to do the *Dakṣiṇāmūrti stotram*. That also took about three such gatherings, each lasting three days. We did not finish that text, for Swami Advayananda was appointed Ācārya, Sandeepany Mumbai. We will resume this activity when he completes his course in 2013.

Brahmacārī Atharvana Chaitanya, Ācārya, CM Ahmedabad

The five-day Ācāryas' Conference at Kolwan in 2009 with its group discussions was a very beneficial experience. Prior to the conference, we were given four topics on Vedānta that, we were told, would be the topics of discussion in the various groups into which we would be divided. The division of the groups was based on language and I was in an English-speaking group. Each group had about fifteen to twenty Ācāryas and we would meet for a one-hour discussion every day. On each day we had a fresh topic to discuss.

Several Ācāryas are very learned people with a deep understanding of our scriptures. So there was erudition, and there was also a wealth of references and examples, which were particularly useful for junior Ācāryas like me. Some of the perspectives that were shared really opened my eyes to the many different ways in which one can see and understand a single idea from the scriptures. Time, however, was limited, and everyone in the group was a speaker! So, it was quite a challenge to be crisp, brief, and to the point.

What many of us appreciated was the fact that novices and seniors discussed topics as equals. Normally we are used to looking at the seniors seated on the dais, discoursing; but here we were all sitting together doing mananam on the same topic. That gave all of us a feeling of oneness. It not only enabled us to better understand each other, but also to deeply appreciate the others.

Swamini Supriyananda, Ācārya, CM Hong Kong

When I teach, I like to make sure that I cater to all ages and varieties of aspiring learners. People learn differently. The CHYKs, especially, seem to enjoy a discussion/Study Group type of environment. They learn better when mentally stimulated by thought-provoking questions and active discussion about the logic and principles of Vedānta. I enjoy facilitating Study Groups because it is nice to see people discover things through logical thought patterns. In these classes, I make sure I don't talk, but I just keep asking lots of questions.

Today, when I meet the youth who were in my class, I can really appreciate the benefit of the Study Group. I can see how strong their foundation is. The method of discussing and arriving at conclusions through active effort and not by just passively hearing the teacher has, indeed, strengthened their conviction and confidence in the concepts. They are able to apply the logic and use what they have learned to answer many other questions. Truly, Gurudev's Grace flows to every single person who reads his words on the pages of the books he wrote.

Ācārya Vilasini, *CM Washington Regional Center, Washington, D.C.*

Study Groups have declined in number in the U.S. since the 1980s when more Ācāryas came to the U.S., but they are still extremely relevant and beneficial for those wishing to learn Vedānta. In the early days, Gurudev or another Swami would come and teach a Vedānta scripture, and then advise us to continue personal reflection in a Chinmaya Study Group. Study Groups were thus an extremely important component of study. Furthermore, they enhance the satsaṅga atmosphere of learning together and supporting one's sādhanā. Attending a Vedānta class does not create that same personal involvement.

In Chinmaya Mission Washington Regional Center (CMWRC), we have talked for years about how to promote Study Groups within the context of a large Mission, with several Ācāryas teaching classes. What we saw is that, as more Ācāryas came to teach, the numbers of Vedānta classes increased. People had to make a choice between a Study Group or a class, because, given the time constraints here with work, raising children, and so on, most people cannot devote two days per week to spiritual activity. For that one day a week, the Mission generally promotes classes. There are some Chinmaya centers, however, that do promote Study Groups, and others, like Washington, where there is a good mix of both Study Groups and classes.

Washington, D.C., 1988. Members of an early Study Group and key sevaks of CMWRC. Sitting/kneeling L to R – Mrs. J. K. Sarma, Vilasini, Gurudev, Ashlesha Tamboli, Veronica Hausman. Standing L to R – J. K. Sarma, Sreedevi Kumar, unknown, Suresh Balakrishnan, Nanik Lahori, M. S. Rao, Balan, Vijay Kumar.

For many years, I put my energy into starting and leading Study Groups. But, at some point, I preferred to teach classes instead, perhaps for my own sake. I had to decide whether or not a class or a Study Group was going to be better for the students. In other words, did they need śravaṇam or mananam? Perhaps one option would be for Ācāryas to give yajñas for śravaṇam, and then ensure that regular study for mananam continues in a Study Group. Each Ācārya has to define his or her own role. Generally, there are far fewer Swamis than are needed. So, there is room for both classes and Study Groups; hopefully, both can flourish.

***Brahmacārī Jagrat Chaitanya**, Ācārya, CM Jaffna, Sri Lanka*

Wherever I was posted (Rambodha and now Jaffna), people were not familiar with the Study Group concept. So, initially, it was challenging because, when I did attempt to start Study Groups, members expected me to speak. They would not express their own opinions. Also, they were not regular in attending class. So I had to spend considerable time in explaining the importance of active participation.

Currently, I have four Study Groups in which I am the moderator. In my absence, they do manage, but that is only for short spells. The medium of communication in these groups is Tamil, and most of the group members are government officers and teachers. Personally, I enjoy the Study Group format because I was part of a CHYK Study Group before joining Sandeepany, Mumbai. That association opened my mind to things in life that I would never have thought about otherwise.

***Swami Nikhilananda**, Regional Head, Chinmaya Mission, National Capital Region based in New Delhi*

The Ācārya's role is mainly to give pravacana and to encourage Study Groups. But it is gṛhasthas who must conduct the Study Groups. Unfortunately, people are often hesitant to assume the leadership role. One reason for this is the assumption, in many Indian minds, that spirituality implies passive listening to a Guru. Perhaps it has something to do with our existing system of education where independent thinking and expression of personal ideas and opinions are not always encouraged.

I also feel that the Study Group is not for everyone. You need to be a jijñāsu (a seeker of knowledge) in order to want to really study and understand for yourself. Jijñāsus are invariably fewer in number than śrotās (listeners). If members of a Study Group are not jijñāsus, they will drop out soon enough. What also happens quite often is that they change the format of the class: they introduce more chanting or they watch DVDs. These imply less discussion and independent thinking.

Personally, I find the periodic interaction with our Study Group members very rewarding. Their ability to listen and then ask questions and engage in discussion is what makes the teaching of Vedānta so meaningful and fulfilling.

New Delhi, 2012. Swami Nikhilananda with two Study Groups of Delhi. Seated L to R – Ashima Arora, Anita Raina Thapan, Swami Nikhilananda, Mitul Seth, Nila Kothari. Standing from L to R – Renuka Manchanda, Sumir Chaudhry, Gurinder Singh, Neelam Kapur, Ricky Srivastava, Soumabha Das, Urvashi Mani, Sunamyka Singh, Pooja Bansal.

XXVI

Reflections of Group Sevaks and Members

Vishva Sodhi, London, England

I think the Study Group is more relevant now than ever before. As a young person of Indian heritage living in Europe with all the comfort, choice, and political stability one could ever wish for, I often observe dissatisfaction and a lack of fulfillment among people of my age. My peers seek joy in absolute career fulfillment (which is rare to find) and through the search for a perfect relationship. Many escape the anxiety of modern living through alcohol and indulgent lifestyles or spa breaks. All of us find ourselves on a conveyor belt looking for something without even knowing what it is and where we might find it. The Study Group harnesses the intellectual approach we value in modern times, and sets us on the time-tested path of living a life filled with deeper and subtler joys, directed toward a lofty and meaningful goal.

Really trying to live what we learn demands hard work and going against the grain — that is why meeting weekly with others who are also walking the path deepens our understanding and is critical in sustaining the enthusiasm to continue. I marvel at the fact that a group of youngsters meet every week to learn how to live their lives through Gurudev, in twenty-first-century Britain!

M. S. Gadkary, Mumbai

In Kuwait, we became very dedicated and intense in our study because there was no regular pravacana available because foreigners are not permitted to own property in the country, nor is the propagation of religious activity permitted. So we have the Study Group. Gurudev always said that the *Gītā* is active resistance to evil. So it is not a passive state. And if you are always listening, then you are always passive. By bringing up examples and applying the knowledge to everyday situations, the correct teaching of the scriptures can take place. And that can happen only in a Study Group.

Shibani Khorana, New Delhi

Each one in the Study Group has been special in his or her own way. The quieter ones started speaking; the ones who spoke a lot started thinking more deeply; those who were irregular tried to be regular. Each one was touched by the knowledge. As our Gurus explain, when one goes near fire, one feels hot, for that is the nature of fire; so, too, the nature of this knowledge is such that it blesses one and all.

Hemachandrudu Linga, Chennai

It is wrong to think that the Study Group is a body of amateurs led by an amateur. One does not need to discuss only with very knowledgeable people because, ultimately, every form of knowledge is within us. We only have to trigger the process of thinking. No answer, unless you can already feel it within, will work for you. Every answer is there in the heart and you find it through your own deep reflection. The more you reflect, the more the answers come. That is why Gurudev said that knowledge is given, wisdom is taken. Wisdom comes from you. Discussion does not imply definite conclusions and answers to all doubts. It is not about gaining total clarity. The process of discussion makes you think, and your own thinking leads you to your answers. So the Study Group forum is not about teaching anything to anyone. It is merely to stimulate independent thinking.

Madhuriben Sheth, Mumbai

When you lead a Study Group, the other members look up to you and you have to be worthy of that respect. So you consciously try to make this knowledge your own so that you can live up to what Gurudev expected of his sevaks. He wanted sevaks to show the path to others. If we break down, then we are letting him down.

Prarthana Saran, New Delhi

Gurudev called us his 'soldiers' who would 'march on to the world's darkest corners and illuminate them with the torch of knowledge' that he was handing over to us. At the beautiful convocation ceremony at the closing of the complete *Bhagavad-gītā* course that he had conducted, he brought home the message loud and clear: "When this Swami is no longer in this body, he will continue his work in this world, to spread knowledge through your mouths, and do service through your hands and feet."

Srichand Krishnani, Mumbai

Gurudev said there are three things that are important for the Chinmaya Mission member: exposure, involvement, and commitment. When we listen to the Masters, there is sufficient exposure. When we volunteer to do some activity at the Mission, then there is involvement. The third is commitment, which comes only through the Study Group. Only by discussion can you concretize your thinking, and with that comes conviction, which expresses itself through thoughts, words, and deeds. That is what you gain from the Study Group.

H. P. Ishwar, Mumbai

The Study Group is serious business. To be regular, you have to set priorities and, most importantly, you have got to think. Swami Tejomayananda says you can live without food for many days, without water for some days, without air for a few moments, but, without thinking, you can live your whole life!

Another important aspect of the Study Group is that you learn to discipline yourself and still tolerate indiscipline from others without getting upset. If Gurudev had to manage with people like us, then, likewise, we have to manage with others around us. It is for our own benefit, let's be clear about that.

D. C. Rao, *Washington, D.C., U.S.A.*

The Study Group is effective when the leader knows enough to be able to guide other members of the group. Some people think that it's a democratic-flat-world-kind-of-get-together, but I think that there has to be someone who is *primus inter pares,* who can guide people, correct misunderstandings, raise questions, and so on. Many gṛhasthas do not feel confident doing that because they do not know the scriptures well enough themselves, and they have not done enough personal sādhanā. So they feel reluctant.

Frederick, Maryland, 2012. The Study Group led by D. C. Rao. From L to R clockwise – Sukanya Sathya, D. C. Rao, Bhavani Prasad, Soman Gopalan, B. K. Sathya, Hari Peakasha, Sangamesh, Ramanathan Palaniappan.

The Swamis focus on pravacana, as that is their sādhanā. They have little time to promote the Study Group, and that is why the Study Group has fallen between two stools. But for the gṛhastha, merely listening to talks is not enough.

Padmaja Joshi, *San Francisco Bay Area, California, U.S.A.*

To keep the discipline and to make the discussion meaningful, the moderator has to be a humble devotee of Pūjya Gurudev. He or she must have a plan and should be skilled in sticking to it without insistence and rigidity. The Study Group moderator should have studied well and should know the material and other references. At the same time, he or she must be able to encourage others to bloom from within. Finally, a pleasant, happy smile and a warm, friendly nature always help.

Sonia Sahney, *Toronto, Ontario, Canada*

Rarely do you come across an opportunity to fundamentally change the course of your life. You go from living your life to watching yourself live your life. You go from waiting to talk to actually listening to people. You go from thinking about what others think to examining how you think. You start to choose your thoughts and control your mind. The result? You become more positive, you become more compassionate, you question everything, and you start to solidify what you have always heard but never understood. You start taking abstract concepts, which you never spent time dissecting, and you begin reflecting on them. Then a surprising thing happens — the more you reflect, the more life begins making sense!

Urvashi and Narayan Mani, *New Delhi*

The interactive and informal atmosphere lends itself to deep insights gained in a non-intimidating atmosphere. The choice of texts is very logical — foundational texts followed by books that reinforce core principles.

Margaret Dukes, Toronto, Ontario, Canada

Having been exposed to Vedānta for many years, I had a tendency to use Vedāntic terms when discussing the scriptures and had become a very good parrot. This tendency has now almost stopped, thanks to our Study Group leader who compels us to use our own words when speaking in the group. Our Study Group leader lives the teachings and her life exemplifies that. As Gurudev said, "Spoken words gain no dynamism at all if the speaker himself is not living the meaning of it vitally."

At the core of the Vedāntic teaching is Oneness, and this is what we experience in the Study Group. We understand that even though we all look different on the outside — as Westerners and Easterners — we all want to live happier and more peaceful lives. In the Study Group, because of the subject matter, we draw positive thoughts to ourselves. How to maintain these higher levels of thinking during the rest of the week becomes our 'homework' and a weeklong challenge. The more we live our lives in a contemplative manner, the better prepared we are for the next class. Ever so slowly, the ideas we discuss in class begin to take root in our minds. Thus, it is only natural that, if we sincerely participate in a Study Group, our minds will become more alert and vigilant, and therefore quieter, just as Gurudev said so many times from the platform and in satsaṅga.

Anil Chaudhary, New Delhi

The Study Group, I feel, is the core activity for every Mission member, for it is the one thing that leads to self-development. Other activities are also interesting: They inspire you and you participate in them. But the real growth happens only through the Study Group. One should be part of a Study Group for years together to ensure that there is continuous svādhyāya. Regular reading at home may be good, but it is not the same as being part of a Study Group.

Vishva Sodhi, London, England

My pet cat Cobweb is probably the longest attending and most regular attendee of my mother's Study Group at home. He finds a suitable spot on a Mission member's lap during opening prayers, and sleeps blissfully for an hour-and-a-half. The subtle vibrations and love generated by invoking the Guru and the teachings are so strong — he never misses a class!

London, 2012. Cobweb the cat is a regular attendee of the Study Group led by Smita Samani.

Anita Raina Thapan, New Delhi

For nearly five years, Rustam was a part of the Defence Colony Study Group in New Delhi. Not being allowed into the yoga-cum-satsaṅga hall, he made it a point to sit just outside the door with one paw extended into the room — to include himself in the group. He sat silent and still for the duration of the class. And he always had a special love for Swami Nikhilananda; for Swamiji ensured, whenever he visited, that Rustam, too, got his share of *prasādam* like everyone else. If Rustam could speak, I do believe, his words would be: "I must have done something really good in my previous life to be exposed to this knowledge and to so many mahātmās!"

A member of a London Study Group led by Ramesh Patni

A study class is like a gas station. We need to visit it regularly to replenish the spiritual fuel to ensure that we drive smoothly on our life's journey.

Cauvery Bhalla, Mumbai

Gurudev had the ability to give the common man the courage to talk on the śāstras. He could create teachers. And that process happened through the Study Group. So, for me, the Study Group is the lifeblood of the Mission.

***Christine Grimmer and David Buccholz**, Melbourne, Australia*

After all these years, we still feel that if Swamiji's [Gurudev's] presence can be felt anywhere, it is in the sacred space of the Vedānta Study Group. When even two or three people come together to dive into that most sacred and uniquely liberating study, we can still discover, through Him, a small taste of our own divine nature.

Gurudev once spoke of the importance of preserving 'islands of sanity' in a crazy world. Perhaps this could be the best final description of the true Vedānta Study Group.

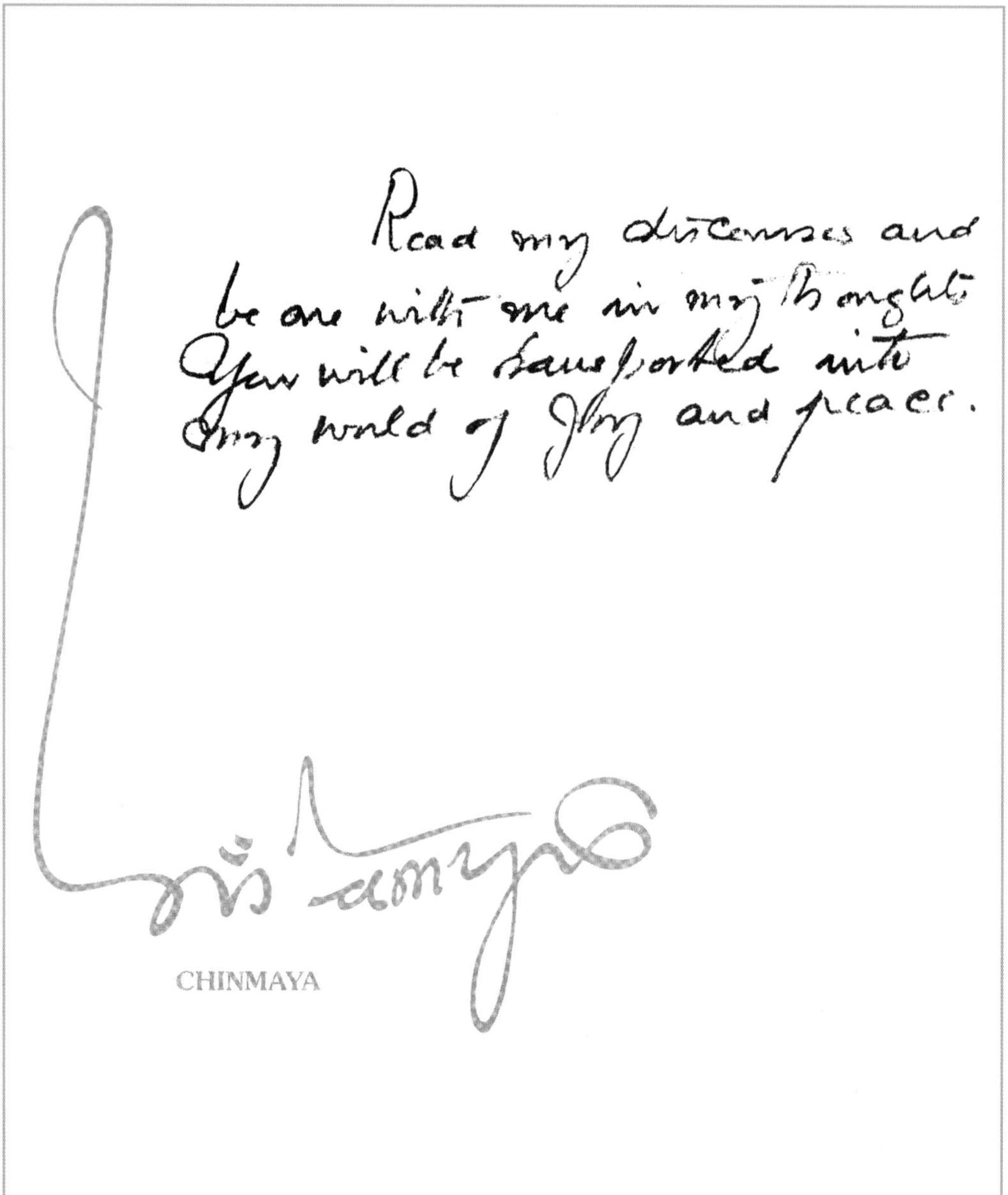

Read my discourses and be one with me in my thoughts. You will be transported into my world of Joy and peace.

CHINMAYA

APPENDIX

Scheme of Study

Scheme of Study for the Study Group

Sequence No.	Title of Text	Dose
1.	Kindle Life	10 pages
2.	Bhaja Govindam	4 stanzas
3.	Tattva Bodhaḥ	5 pages
4.	Manaḥ-śodhanam	2 stanzas
5.	Ātma Bodhaḥ	3 stanzas
6.	Upadeśa-sāra	2 stanzas
7.	Nārada Bhakti Sūtra	5 sūtras
8.	Meditation and Life	1 chapter
9.	Bhagavad-gītā — Introduction, Chapters I and II	10 pages
10.	Jñānasāraḥ	2 stanzas
11.	Kena Upaniṣad	1 mantra
12.	Bhagavad-gītā — Chapter III–VI	3 stanzas
13.	Dhyānasvaūpam	stanzas
14.	Kaivalya Upaniṣad	2 mantras
15.	Bhagavad-gītā Chapters VII–IX	3 stanzas
16.	Īśāvāsya Upaniṣad	3 mantras
17.	Bhagavad-gītā Chapters X–XII	3 stanzas
18.	Bhakti Sudhā	3 stanzas
19.	Gītā, Chapters XIII–XV	3 stanzas
20.	Muṇḍaka Upaniṣad	2 mantras
21.	Gītā, Chapters XVI–XVIII	3 stanzas
22.	Saddarśanam	1 stanza

Scheme of Study For Advanced Study Groups

Sequence No.	Title of Text	Dose
1.	Yoga Vasiṣṭha-sāra-saṅgraha	1 stanza
2.	Advaita Makaranda	2 stanzas
3.	Aitareya Upaniṣad	3 mantras
4.	Dakṣiṇāmūrti-stotram	2 stanzas
5.	Kaṭha Upaniṣad	2 mantras
6.	Praśna Upaniṣad	2 mantras
7.	Taittirīya Upaniṣad	2 mantras
8.	Māṇḍūkya Upaniṣad	2 mantras

Self-Study Books

1.	Vedānta Through Letters	10 pages
2.	We Must	10 pages
3.	Sādhanā Pañcakam	1 stanza
4.	Puruṣa Sūktam	4 mantras
5.	Hymn to Badrīnātha	5 stanzas
6.	Viṣṇu Sahasranāma	3 pages

Self-Study CDs/DVDs

Bhagavad-gītā — Commentary by Gurudev Swami Chinmayananda

Vivekacūḍāmaṇi — Commentary by Gurudev Swami Chinmayananda

Chinmaya Mission Pledge

We stand as one family,
  bound to each other with love and respect.
We serve as an army,
  courageous and disciplined
  ever ready to fight against
  all low tendencies and false values,
  within and without us.
We live honestly
  the noble life of sacrifice and service
  producing more than what we consume
  and giving more than what we take.
We seek the Lord's grace
  to keep us on the path of
  virtue, courage and wisdom.
May Thy Grace and blessings
  flow through us
  to the world around us.
We believe that the service of our country
  is the service of the Lord of Lords
  and devotion to the people
  is the devotion to the Supreme Self.
We know our responsibilities;
  Give us the ability and courage to fulfil them.

Om Tat Sat

Glossary

A	abhyas	practice
	ācārya	Teacher
	arcanā	worship of the Lord
	āśrama	stage of life or a Hindu hermitage
	asuras	demonic beings
	āstika	one who has faith that the Vedas are the valid means of knowledge
	Ātman	the Self, pure Consciousness
	Ātma-jñāna	Knowledge of the Self
	avatāra	divine incarnation
B	bhajan	hymn
	Bhāgavat Saptāha	discourses on the *Śrīmad Bhāgavatam* over seven days
	bhakti	devotion
	Bhārata	the traditional name for India
	bhāṣya	exposition or commentary
	bhikṣā	offering of food to a renunciate
	bindī	red dot applied on the forehead for religious and social purposes
	Brahmacārī	a student of Veda, the first of the four stages of life
	brahmacarya āśrama	the stage of life of a Brahmacārin
	Brahmavidyā	Knowledge of Brahman
	Brahma-sūtra	text of aphorisms on the teachings of the Upaniṣads, authored by Veda Vyāsa
C	catursūtri	four aphorisms from a larger text which convey the essence of the whole text
D	devas	the Gods
	dharma	essential nature of a thing, duty, or righteousness
	Dharma Sevak Course	a six-week immersion course in spiritual living and the knowledge of Vedānta in order to better serve the cause of the mission
	dhyāna yoga	the Path of meditation

	dakṣiṇā	an offering to the priest or Teacher; also called Guru dakṣiṇā
G	gandha	faculty of smell
	gāyatrī-havana	a fire ritual accompanied by the repetition of the Gāyatrī
	gṛhastha	householder; the second of the four stages of life
	Gītācārya	the Teacher of the *Gītā*, i.e., Lord Kṛṣṇa
	guṇa	property, quality
	gurukula	a traditional school, traditional residential school
	Guru-dakṣiṇā	a token of gratitude offered by a student to the teacher upon completion of studies
	Guru-śiṣya-paramparā	lineage of teachers and disciples
I	Īśvara	the Lord
	Iṣṭa devatā	a devotee's chosen deity
J	jagadguru	literally, world spiritual teacher; usually, an honorific title
	jagat	creation, world
	japa	continuous chanting of Lord's name
	jalpa	wrangling discussion or debate
	jijñāsu	seeker of knowledge
	jīva	the individual
	jñāna yajña	a series of lectures on Vedānta; also referred to as yajña
	jñāna-yoga	the Path of knowledge
	jñānī	Man of Wisdom, one who is Self-realized
K	karma bhūmi	field of selfless service
	karma kāṇḍa	portion of Vedas dealing with rituals
	Kārikā	commentary
	Khudā	a word derived from Farsi, which means 'God.' It was incorporated into the Urdu and Hindustani languages
M	mahāsamādhi	end of physical being of a spiritual Master
	mālā	rosary; also called japa mālā
	mananam	reflection on the scriptures
	maṭha	monastic institution
	Māyā	cosmic delusory power of the Lord; illusion
	mokṣa	liberation from the cycle of birth and death

	mūrti	idol of the Lord
N	nāma	the sacred name of the Lord
	nāstika	one who does not accept the authority of the Vedas
	nididhyāsana	contemplation on the nature of the Self
P	pādukā pūjā	worship of the Guru's sandals
	pārāyaṇa	daily recitation or reading of the scriptures
	paramparā	lineage
	pāṭhaśālā	traditional Indian school
	pracāraka	one who works for the spread of knowledge
	prakaraṇa grantha	introductory texts that explain concepts of Vedānta for lay persons
	prasāda	an offering made to a deity or saint and then distributed as blessings
	pravacanam	discourse on the scriptures
	pūjā	ritualistic worship
	pujārī	priest in a temple
	Pūjya	who is worthy of worship
R	rajas	one of the three thought textures (guṇas); it is characterized by activity, passion, and agitation
	rasa	flavor, feeling, essence
	Ṛṣī	Sage
	rūpa	form
S	ṣad-sampatti	the six virtues necessary for a seeker: *śama* (control of the mind), *dama* (control of the senses), *uparama* (balance of mind), titīkṣā (forbearance), *śraddhā* (faith) and *samādhāna* (single-pointed attention)
	sādhanā	spiritual practice or discipline
	sādhaka	one who practices spiritual disciplines
	samādhi	complete absorption of mind in meditation
	samaṣṭi	the macrocosm as opposed to vyaṣṭi or microcosm
	saṁskāras	inclinations, innate tendencies
	śānti pāṭha	peace invocation
	sannyāsī	ascetic, renunciate
	sannyāsa	the path of renunciation; the fourth and last stage of life

	Śāradā pīṭha	first of the four Hindu monastic orders established by Ādi Śaṅkarācārya at Sringeri in the state of Karnataka
	śāstra	text pertaining to a particular knowledge, scripture
	śāstra sadas	discussion forum for those who are learned in the scriptures
	satī	self-immolation by a widow on the funeral pyre of her husband
	satsaṅga	company of the wise and pure
	sattva	one of the three thought textures (guṇas); expresses as knowledge and serenity
	satyam	truth, truthfulness
	sevā	service done in a spirit of selflessness
	sevak/sevikā	one who serves
	śloka	a verse
	smṛti	literally means 'remembered.' Works based on the wisdom of the Vedas authored by enlightened individuals, unlike the 'śruti' that was 'revealed' to Ṛṣīs in moments of deep meditation. Smṛti also includes traditional law and social norms based on the Vedas
	śravaṇam	listening to the scriptures
	śrotā	one who listens
	Śruti	Vedas
	stotram	hymn of praise
	sūtra	aphorism
	svādhyāya	study of the scriptures by which one can strengthen spiritual understanding and awareness; study of one's own nature and personality
	svabhāva	one's inherent nature and inclinations
T	tapas	austerity
	tamas	one of the three thought textures (guṇas); expresses as ignorance and stupor
	ṭīkā	commentary on Śaṅkara bhāṣya (the commentary of Śaṅkara)
	tyāgī	renunciate
U	Upaniṣads	portion of the Vedas that pertain to knowledge of the Self

	upāsanā kāṇḍa	portion of the Vedas that pertains to spiritual practice and worship
	upāsanā	spiritual practice, worship
V	vāda	a system of scholarly debate with logic
	Vaikuṇṭha	the Supreme abode of Lord Viṣṇu
	Vaiśvānara	the all-pervading consciousness or Supreme Being, also an epithet for fire
	vairāgya	detachment, dispassion vānaprastha āśrama third stage of life when one withdraws from worldly duties
	vāsanā	habitual tendencies, impressions gained from past actions
	vibhooti	glory
	vicāra	inquiry into the Self or Truth
	Vijñāna mandir classes	scriptural classes
	Viṣṇu sahasranāma	the 1,000 names of Lord Viṣṇu
	vitaṇḍa	destructive criticism
	vyaṣṭi	the microcosm as opposed to samaṣṭi or macrocosm
Y	yajña	a ritual sacrifice or offering
	yajña prasāda	blessings from the yajña
	yajñaśālā	place where the yajña is performed
	Yuva Veer	youth who has undergone the Youth Empowerment Program (YEP) run by Chinmaya Yuva Kendra

Patrons and Contributors

Grateful acknowledgement and special thanks are given to the following:

CHINMAYA MISSION DELHI

| NEW DELHI, INDIA |

CHINMAYA MISSION CHICAGO

| WILLOWBROOK, ILLINOIS, U.S.A. |

FULL CIRCLE PUBLISHING

| NEW DELHI, INDIA |

DAVID & MARGARET DUKES

| TORONTO, ONTARIO, CANADA |

ARUN & RASHMI MEHROTRA

| NAPERVILLE, ILLINOIS, U.S.A. |

TRANSLITERATION AND PRONUNCIATION GUIDE

In the book, Devanāgarī characters are transliterated according to the scheme adopted by the International Congress of Orientalists at Athens in 1912. In it, one fixed pronunciation value is given to each letter; f, q, w, x, and z are not called to use. An audio recording of this guide is available at www.chinmayamission.com/scriptures.php. According to this scheme:

	sounds like		*sounds like*
a	o in s*o*n	ḍh	dh in a*dh*esive
ā	a in f*a*ther	ṇ	n in u*n*der*
i	i in d*i*fferent	t	t in *t*abla
ī	ee in f*ee*l	th	th in *th*umb
u	u in f*u*ll	d	th in *th*is
ū	oo in b*oo*t	dh	dh in Gan*dh*i
ṛ	rh in *rh*ythm*	n	n in *n*ose
ṝ	**	p	p in *p*en
ḷ	**	ph	ph in *ph*antom*
e	a in ev*a*de	b	b in *b*oil
ai	i in del*i*ght	bh	bh in a*bh*or
o	o in c*o*re	m	m in *m*ind
au	o in n*o*w	y	y in *y*es
k	c in *c*alm	r	r in *r*ight
kh	kh in *kh*an	l	l in *l*ove
g	g in *g*ate	v	v in *v*ery
gh	gh in *gh*ost	ś	sh in *sh*ut
ṅ	an in *an*kle*	ṣ	s in *s*ugar
c	ch in *ch*uckle	s	s in *s*imple
ch	ch in wit*ch**	h	h in *h*appy
j	j in *j*ustice	ṁ	m in i*m*provise
jh	jh in *Jh*ansi	ḥ	**
ñ	ny in ba*ny*an	kṣ	tio in ac*tio*n
ṭ	t in *t*ank	tr	th in *th*ree*
ṭh	**	jñ	gn in *gn*osis
ḍ	d in *d*og	'	a silent 'a'

* These letters do not have an exact English equivalent. An approximation is given here.
** These sounds cannot be approximated in English words.